American Book Company's

MASTERING THE

Georgia 3rd Grade CRCT

in

Reading

Aligned to the New Georgia Performance Standards (GPS)

Kim Hill
Dr. Karen Michael
Zuzana Urbanek
Project Director: Dr. Frank J. Pintozzi

American Book Company
PO Box 2638
Woodstock, GA 30188-1383
Toll Free: 1 (888) 264-5877   Phone: (770) 928-2834
Fax: (770) 928-7483   Toll Free Fax: 1 (866) 827-3240
www.americanbookcompany.com

ACKNOWLEDGEMENTS

The authors would like to gratefully acknowledge the formatting contributions of Yvonne Benson and Marsha Torrens, as well as the editing contributions of Margaret DuPree and Dr. Frank Pintozzi. Charisse Johnson was the graphics illustrator for this book.

This product/publication includes images from CorelDRAW 9 and 11 which are protected by the copyright laws of the United States, Canada, and elsewhere. Used under license.

Table of Contents

3R3h

Georgia 3rd Grade CRCT in Reading
Preface

Mastering the Georgia 3rd Grade CRCT in Reading will help students who are learning or reviewing the GPS standards for the Reading sections of the **Georgia 3rd Grade CRCT in Reading**. The materials in this book are based on the GPS standards as published by the Georgia Department of Education.

This book contains several sections:

      1) General information about the book itself

      2) A diagnostic test

      3) An evaluation chart

      4) Fourteen chapters that teach the concepts and skills needed for test readiness

      5) Two practice tests

Standards are posted at the beginning of each chapter, in the diagnostic and practice tests, and in a chart included in the answer manual.

We welcome comments and suggestions about this book. Please contact the Project Coordinator at

American Book Company
PO Box 2638
Woodstock, GA 30188-1383

Call Toll Free: (888) 264-5877
Phone: (770) 928-2834
Toll Free Fax: 1 (866) 827-3240

Visit us online at
www.americanbookcompany.com

Preface

About the Authors:

Kim Hill graduated magna cum laude from Kennesaw State University and taught English and Language Arts. She currently works with at-risk students on the elementary reading level.

Karen H. Michael has been teaching for 17 years. Dr. Michael completed her doctorate at Purdue University in 2002 in literacy and language education. Since 2000, she is an assistant professor in the Tift College of Education at Mercer University. She has four publications and has made more than 25 presentations at local, regional, and international conferences. Dr. Michael has trained many elementary and middle school language arts/reading teachers in Georgia, South Carolina, and Indiana through professional development courses.

About the Project Coordinator:

Zuzana Urbanek serves as ELA Curriculum Coordinator for American Book Company. She is a professional writer with 25 years of experience in education, business, and publishing. She has taught a variety of English courses since 1990 at the college level and also taught English as a foreign language abroad. Her master's degree is from Arizona State University.

About the Project Director:

Dr. Frank J. Pintozzi is a former professor of Education at Kennesaw (GA) State University. For over 28 years, he has taught English and reading at the high school and college levels as well as in teacher preparation courses in language arts and social studies. In addition to writing and editing state standard-specific texts for high school exit and end of course exams, he has edited and written numerous college textbooks.

Georgia 3rd Grade CRCT in Reading
Diagnostic Test

The purpose of this diagnostic test is to measure your knowledge in reading comprehension. This diagnostic test is based on the Georgia Performance Standards for Reading and adheres to the sample question format provided by the Georgia Department of Education.

General Directions:

1. Read all directions carefully.

2. Read each question or sample. Then choose the best answer.

3. Choose only one answer for each question. If you change an answer, be sure to erase your original answer completely.

4. After taking the test, you or your instructor should score it using the evaluation chart following the test. This will enable you to determine your strengths and weaknesses.

All About Mitch

Mitch was tall and skinny. He had red hair and was covered with freckles. He was also very intelligent. Last year, he won the school math contest and was given a gold trophy. He played soccer on a team called Ireland at the YMCA. Mitch liked basketball too. As soon as he got home from school, he completed his homework. His teacher assigned homework every day, but even on days when she forgot, Mitch still practiced his math and reading skills. Then, he'd play ball in the yard with his dad.

1. Which word means the same as the word *skinny*?   3R2C
   A. tall   B. thin   C. smart   D. short

2. Where did Mitch play soccer?   3R3J
   A. at the YMCA
   B. in Ireland
   C. in the yard
   D. at school

3. Mitch was   3R3F
   A. short, chubby, and smart.
   B. tall, skinny, and clumsy.
   C. tall, skinny, and intelligent.
   D. short, athletic, and kind.

4. What did Mitch and his dad do after Mitch finished his homework?   3R3J
   A. ate dinner
   B. walked around the block
   C. played ball in the yard
   D. practiced soccer

Dad's Special Box

Brian has been told not to play in his parents' bedroom time and time again. Brian wanted to look in his dad's special box on the top of his dresser. Brian went into the room and reached up high and got the special box. Oh no! He got scared and dropped the box. Everything inside the special box fell out. Brian thought he picked up everything, but he missed a gold coin that rolled under the dresser. When his dad came home, he asked Brian what he had been up to that afternoon. Brian told his dad that he had been riding his bike.

5. What happened first in the story?   3R3E
   A. Brian got the special box.
   B. Brian put the special box back on his dad's dresser.
   C. Brian picked up everything but the gold coin.
   D. Brian rode his bike.

6. How will Brian's dad know that Brian told a lie?   3R3L
   A. He will see that the box is broken.
   B. He will discover that the gold coin is missing.
   C. He will see that the box is on the floor.
   D. He will see that the box has disappeared.

7. Brian was asked not to do something. What was it?   3R3J
   A. Brian was not supposed to ride his bike.
   B. Brian was not supposed to play in his parent's bedroom.
   C. Brian was not supposed to eat cereal from the cereal box.
   D. Brian was not supposed to do his homework.

8. What is the opposite of the word *special*?   3R3C
   A. unique   B. unusual   C. plain   D. extraordinary

Moving Day

It was spring in Georgia, and the Hubbard family was very happy. They were moving to a new house. "Please, oh please," Will asked his mom, "can we take the tree house?" Will had spent many hours building a tree house in the back yard. He loved the tree house, especially the trap door. Will's mom was busy packing, and she said, "Go ask your dad what can be done, if anything." Will's dad was loading the moving van. "Please, oh please," Will said, "can we take the tree house?"

"There's no way to move all that wood, son," said his father firmly.

Will cried out, "It's not fair! It's just not fair! You get to take your stuff!"

Will walked back in the house, slamming the door behind him on purpose.

"We must all leave things behind," Will's mom said softly. "I am so sorry. I can't take my prize roses. They won't make the trip. The roses will die if I remove them from the dirt." The next morning the Hubbard family left for their new home. Will and his mom had agreed to work outside every day that spring. They were going to plant roses and build a new tree house.

9. In what season does the story take place?   3R3M
   A. winter   B. fall   C. summer   D. spring

10. What did Will's mom have to leave behind?   3R3J
    A. her favorite chair
    B. her special garden
    C. her books
    D. her prize roses

11. What did Will have to leave behind?   3R3G
    A. his books
    B. his favorite chair
    C. his tree house
    D. his wooded back yard

12. Where does the Hubbard family live? 3R3M
    A. Texas
    B. Georgia
    C. California
    D. North Carolina

---

13. Which of these words means "to carry or support" or " a large, meat-eating mammal"? 3R2B
    A. haul   B. bear   C. tiger   D. lug

14. What is the **suffix** in the word transformers? 3R2E
    A. tr   B. trans   C. form   D. ers

15. What is the **root** in the word *transformers*? 3R2E
    A. trans   B. transform   C. form   D. formers

16. Which of the following statements is a fact, not an opinion? 3R3D
    A. I really like my new bike helmet.
    B. It's streamlined and very light.
    C. I guess Mom doesn't worry about me as much.
    D. Probably, she thinks it looks cool, too!

Your Feet Stink!

Do you ever wonder if your feet stink? Do you know that your feet stink? What makes your feet stink? Sweat eating bacteria are what makes your feet stink. The bacteria are attracted to the sweat on your feet, and they like to eat it. Ew! The bacteria have a strong odor that makes your feet smell bad. Your feet have over 200,000 sweat glands. Socks and shoes do not help because that traps the sweat to your skin. Bacteria love dark and damp places. The more you sweat, the more your feet will smell.

Some people believe that the only way to get rid of stinky feet is to wash your shoes, which can harbor odors, dirt, and fungus. You can throw most non-leather shoes into a washing machine with a little bit of laundry detergent and baking soda to eliminate the smell. Any lingering odors can be eliminated with foot powder sprinkled into your shoes daily to prevent bacteria.

How can you prevent the problem?

1 Always wear clean socks.

2 Try to choose shoes that are made of breathable fabrics.

3 You can spray a deodorizer in your shoes. This is especially important for sneakers.

4 Wash your feet every day.

17. Which one of the following statements is an opinion and not a fact? 3R3D
  A. Feet have over 200,000 sweat glands.
  B. Washing your shoes will get rid of stinky feet.
  C. Sweat eating bacteria cause feet to stink.
  D. Bacteria like to grow in damp, dark places.

18. What causes a person's feet to smell? 3R3L
  A. wearing shoes
  B. wearing shoes without socks
  C. bacteria
  D. wearing sandals

19. Which is NOT a solution to stop feet from smelling? 3R3J
  A. wearing clean socks
  B. using a deodorizer
  C. washing feet daily
  D. going barefoot every day

20. The passage "Your Feet Stink" is what kind of writing?   3R3N
    A. fiction   B. poetry   C. biography   D. nonfiction

21. What is the summary of this passage?   3R3G
    A. a description of why people's feet sometimes have an odor
    B. a list of ways to prevent feet from smelling
    C. a list of ways that foot odor happens
    D. an explanation why people wear clean socks and shoes

22. What are favorable conditions for bacteria? Choose the BEST answer for   3R3L
your response.
    A. sweaty feet, dark and damp places
    B. clean feet
    C. leather shoes
    D. dark and damp places

Jewelry Workers

It was 4,500 years ago when the Chinese discovered pearls in oysters. Inside an oyster's shell, there is a special coating that is called mother-of-pearl. Sometimes, a grain of sand gets caught inside the shell. The oyster then covers the grain of sand with layers and layers of mother-of-pearl. The oyster does this to protect itself from getting scratched by the grain of sand. It works hard to make the grain soft and smooth and silky. Over time, that grain of sand becomes a pearl. It takes an oyster about two to four years to make a good size pearl. Pearls are used to make jewelry like earrings, necklaces, and bracelets.

23. What is the beginning of a pearl?   3R3J
    A. sea salt
    B. a grain of sand
    C. an oyster
    D. a pebble

24. Who discovered pearls in oysters?   3R3M
   A. Cherokee Tribe
   B. Irish
   C. Chinese
   D. Creek Tribe

25. What is the special coating that the oyster makes to protect itself?   3R3J
   A. father-of-pearl
   B. mother-of-pearl
   C. pearl earrings
   D. sand pearls

26. The passage "Jewelry Workers" is   3R3N
   A. nonfiction   B. fiction   C. biography   D. poetry

27. How long does it take for an oyster to create one pearl?   3R3M
   A. one to two years
   B. two to four years
   C. 4,500 years
   D. 450 years

_____

28. Many ships and airplanes have *vanished* when entering the Bermuda Triangle.   3R2F
   There has been no sign of people, ships, or airplanes that have ever been
   found in this area of the ocean. Another word for *vanished* is
   A. disappeared.   B. arrived.   C. confused.   D. exploded.

29. Karen is really hungry. She ate a banana, but it did not *appease* her hunger.   3R2F
   Karen now wants to eat something else. What does *appease* probably mean?
   A. annoy   B. satisfy   C. increase   D. eat

30. In the word *unsuccessful*, what is the prefix? 3R2E

    A. un   B. succ   C. success   D. ful

31. In the word *unsuccessful*, what is the root word? 3R2E

    A. un   B. succ   C. success   D. ful

32. In the word *unsuccessful*, what is the suffix? 3R2E

    A. un   B. succ   C. success   D. ful

A Day at the Fair

Characters
Jill, a 13-year-old girl
Traci, her best friend

Act 1, Scene 1
[The two girls are talking in Jill's room.]

JILL [daydreaming while staring out the window]: I love it when the fair comes to town. We've been saving up our allowances for weeks getting ready. I can't wait to spend it all!

TRACI [sitting on Jill's bed]: I love the corn dogs the best.

JILL: I'd rather eat cotton candy and popcorn.

TRACI: But we both like to ride all the rides, even the scary ones.

[The girls laugh.]

TRACI: I can't wait to see how our pumpkin does in the contest we entered at the fair.

JILL [jumping on the bed next to Traci]: It's huge! Last week, it weighed 317 pounds!

TRACI: That's great, but you know… [she looks at Jill as though she is about to break bad news to her] …last year's winner was Mr. Lewis. His pumpkin weighed 502 pounds.

JILL [rolling her eyes]: I nearly hit the roof when I laid eyes on that gigantic pumpkin! But, you know, it was mostly orange but one side was covered with green bumps. Our pumpkin is perfectly orange and it doesn't have a sit spot.

TRACI [making a face at her]: A sit spot?

JILL: You know! A sit spot is what happens when the pumpkin lies on the ground too long and that section gets flat. I made up that word!

TRACI [giggling]: Whatever. Anyway, I think we have a good chance. We take such good care of our pumpkin, like feeding it by injecting milk directly into the vine.

JILL: Oh, and did you hear? If we win the contest, my parents are going to give us three dollars to ride even more rides and eat even more junk food at the fair. Maybe you can get your parents to do the same thing!

TRACI: I'll try! When we get to the fair, let's ride the roller coasters first. Let's save the ferris wheel as a celebration for after we win.

JILL [giving Traci a high-five]: Excellent! I can't wait until the fair gets to town!

33. The word *injecting* in the last paragraph MOST LIKELY means
    A. spooning.   B. sticking.   C. running.   D. milking.

3R2F

34. Which genre is this reading passage?
    A. drama   B. nonfiction   C. biography   D. poetry

3R3N

35. Why did someone write this text?

    A. to educate readers about growing pumpkins

    B. to convince kids that roller coasters are fun

    C. to inform everyone that the fair is coming

    D. to entertain people with an enjoyable story

3R3P

36. What are the two friends going to do if they win the contest?   3R3B, L
    A. have a party
    B. ride the ferris wheel
    C. ride a roller coaster
    D. visit the pumpkin

37. What is Traci's favorite food to eat at the fair?   3R3J
    A. popcorn
    B. corn dog
    C. cotton candy
    D. candy apple

38. Why do you think the friends will win the contest?   3R3F
    A. They talk to the pumpkin.
    B. They rotate the pumpkin and feed it milk.
    C. They planted a good seed.
    D. They water it daily, and it is all orange.

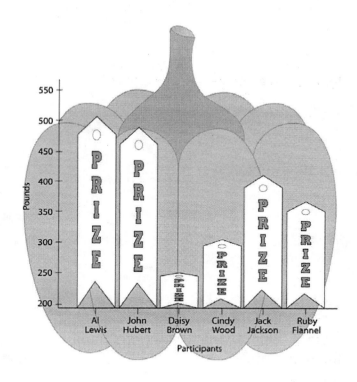

39. At the fair last year, who came in second place?

    A. Miss Daisy Brown

    B. Mr. John Hubert

    C. Mrs. Cindy Wood

    D. Miss Ruby Flannel

40. The OPPOSITE of the word *failure* is
    A. hopeful.   B. success.   C. pride.   D. worthy.

41. The OPPOSITE of the word *partial* is
    A. complete.   B. limited.   C. half.   D. unfair.

42. Paul *talked* to his brother, Peter, about the new boat.
    What is a synonym for the word *talked*?

    A. yelled   B. whispered   C. spoke   D. screamed

43. Lavern wanted a *large* piece of birthday cake with a red rose on top.   3R2C
    What is a synonym for the word *large*?

    A. small   B. big   C. medium   D. teeny

44. Homographs have the same spelling but the words have two different   3R2B, C
    meanings. Which word means "a quacking animal" or "a move downward to
    avoid something"?
    A. bend over   B. duck   C. quick   D. duke

You'd Better Watch Out!

If you are headed down Briarwood Drive past the railroad tracks, be careful and stay away from Mr. Crabapple's house. You can't see his house from the street because there are so many large bushes and thick tree trunks. Once a neighbor was bitten by a raccoon that had his home right there in the front yard. It was the perfect place because the yard was so dense with leaves, tree stumps, and pine cones. Only one window is visible from the edge of Briarwood Drive. The house looks empty, but Mr. Crabapple lives there alone.

Mr. Crabapple is creepy and has this weird way of looking at you. He walks slowly and his hands are gnarled. He always wears blue jeans, an old white T-shirt, and a fishing hat. He smokes a pipe and waves the pipe in the air for no reason at all. Not many people visit him. He's outside quite often, but you can't tell he did anything to his yard. The neighbors make jokes about missing pets being hidden in Mr. Crabapple's yard.

The good thing about Mr. Crabapple is that he always has brownies for us if we dare to go in his yard to talk to him. No one visits him alone. Not even my brother John, who would do just about anything, would even think about going in the yard alone. It is very scary, but we love the brownies. One hot summer day, my friends–Samantha, Emma, and Blake–and my brother, and I were trying to stay out of trouble. We were bored to death and burning up from the hot sun beating down on our backs. Old Man Crabapple was on his front porch. Maybe he will invite us in for a treat! In unison we all screamed, "Brownies!"

We began walking in front of Mr. Crabapple's house. From the sidewalk, we barely could see the house behind all the trees and bushes. Samantha couldn't even open the gate because vines were entwined around the latch. Mr. Crabapple looked up sternly, "What do you be wantin' today?" Then he gave out a bellowing laugh deep from the bottom of his throat. "Would you all like some brownies?," he asked. "Oh yes, sir, we sure would, if it is not too much trouble for you," I replied.

He stood up and got caught in the purple wisteria hanging from the porch. We all scrambled because there were so many bumblebees flying around the sweetsmelling flowers. I hate bees. One came right up in front of my face. I swished it away, but it came right back. "Be still," hollered Emma. I tried, but it is so difficult to be still when a bumblebee is flying right in front of your face. Finally, it flew away.

Mr. Crabapple turned and went into the house. He had been gone awhile, and we were scared that something had happened. We wondered what had taken so long, but we quickly forgot about everything when we saw the delectable brownies. They were stacked like a pyramid on a bright red plastic tray. Blake ate his entire brownie before the rest of us even finished our first bite. It tasted so good in my mouth. The velvet chocolate was so yummy. We each thanked Mr. Crabapple for his hospitality and ran back to my house. It was getting late in the day and John and I had to be home before the streetlights came on or momma would go into one of her panic attacks. Momma was in the kitchen just beginning to set the table for supper. We could smell homemade meatloaf and mashed potatoes. Momma asked us where we had been. When we told her about our visit, she turned pale and had a look of horror on her face. "What's the matter with you? You look like you've seen a ghost," I asked. "I haven't seen a ghost, but I think you have. Mr. Crabapple died last Tuesday, boys," momma exclaimed. My brother and I just stared at each other for a long time. We were too afraid to move. The next time you are on Briarwood Drive, do not stop at Mr. Crabapple's house, no matter how good his brownies are.

45. Describe the setting of this story? 3R3E
    A. a mountain vacation home
    B. an apartment on Wood Road
    C. a house on Briarwood Drive
    D. near railroad tracks

46. How did the brothers feel at the end of the story? 3R3F
    A. angry
    B. happy
    C. scared
    D. tired

---

47. What word sounds the same as *meet*? 3R2C
    A. magic
    B. metal
    C. meat
    D. marker

Summer Morning

The birds chirp with first morning light

The once dark land unfolds

Little orange flowers smile with the dawn

As the flying fairies prance about

Singing their sweet song

All the purple clovers stand

Green coats of moss cover rocks

The fairies lead me down the narrow road

Leading the way to the apple grove

Down where croaks the toad

Wild strawberries reach toward the sun

I find dew on the garden gate

I see the bright blue forget-me-nots and stout pink snapdragons

The garden is bloomin' its magic

Mornin' beams the sun

48. The passage "Summer Morning" is
    A. fiction.
    B. biography.
    C. science report.
    D. poetry.

3R3N

49. What happens first in this passage?
    A. The garden is bloomin' its magic
    B. Wild strawberries reach toward the sun
    C. The birds chirp with first morning light
    D. The fairies lead me down the narrow path

3R3J

50. What is the author's purpose?
    A. to describe a summer morning
    B. to tell about a factual event
    C. to write about a vegetable garden
    D. to describe how birds chirp

3R3P

EVALUATION CHART FOR GEORGIA 3RD GRADE READING CRCT DIAGNOSTIC TEST

Directions: On the following chart, circle the question numbers that you answered incorrectly, and evaluate the results. Then turn to the appropriate chapters, read the explanations, and complete the exercises. Review other chapters as needed. Finally, complete the post-test(s) to assess your progress and further prepare you for the **Georgia 3rd Grade Reading CRCT**.

Note: Some question numbers will appear under multiple chapters because those questions require demonstration of multiple skills.

Chapter	Diagnostic Test Question(s)
Chapter 1: Main Idea and Supporting Details	2, 4, 7, 9, 10, 12, 22, 23, 24, 25, 27, 37, 49
Chapter 2: Summarizing, Predicting, & Inferring	3, 9, 11, 18, 19, 21, 23, 35
Chapter 3: Making Judgments & Drawing Conclusions	3, 22, 38
Chapter 4: Author's Purpose–Why Write this Stuff Anyway?	35, 50
Chapter 5: Cause & Effect	6, 19, 36
Chapter 6: Is It a Fact?	16, 17
Chapter 7: Context Clues and Multiple Meanings	13, 28, 29, 44
Chapter 8: Words–Roots, Prefixes, & Suffixes	14, 15, 30, 31, 32
Chapter 9: Words–Homonyms, Synonyms, & Antonyms	1, 8, 33, 40, 41, 42, 43, 44, 47
Chapter 10: Understanding Genres–Fiction and Nonfiction	20, 26, 45, 46
Chapter 11: Understanding Genres–Drama	34
Chapter 12: Understanding Genres–Poetry	48
Chapter 13: Character, Plot, & Setting	5, 38, 45, 46
Chapter 14: Finding Information in Graphics	39

Chapter 1
Main Idea and Supporting Details

This chapter covers Georgia standard

ELA3R3-j	Identifies and infers main idea and supporting details.

In this chapter, we will learn how to answer questions like those on the CRCT in Reading. The CRCT will test how well you understand what you read. You will see questions like these:

- "What is this passage about?"

- "What is the main idea?"

- "Which supporting details hold up that main idea?"

Once you know how to answer these questions, you will know what to expect on the test. So, let's get started!

MAIN IDEA—THE BIG IDEA

The **main idea** is what a passage is all about. It is the "big idea" of the passage. When you read, ask yourself: "What is this passage about? What is it trying to say?"

You probably already understand main idea without even knowing it. Main ideas are part of your daily life. For example, why do you play with friends? You play because it's fun. This is the main reason (main idea) you do it. Why do you go to the doctor? The main reason (main idea) you go to the doctor is to stay healthy.

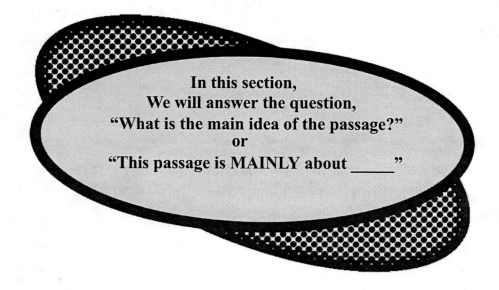

In this section,
We will answer the question,
"What is the main idea of the passage?"
or
"This passage is MAINLY about _____"

It is easy to find the main idea. Sometimes you can find the main idea in the title. For example, read this title.

> What I Did for Summer Vacation

What will this passage be about? Most likely, it will tell what the writer did over the summer. The title shows the "big idea" of the passage.

Other times, the main idea is a sentence. This sentence can be at the beginning or at the end of the passage. For example, say you read a passage about baseball. It tells what happens in the game. The last sentence says, "Baseball is a great sport." This sentence tells you that the main idea is how great baseball is.

Now that we know a little more about main idea, let's practice.

Practice 1: Main Idea

ELA3R3-j

Read the passages and choose the main idea. The first one has been done for you.

Earthworms

Earthworms are really neat animals. They are slimy and have no legs. They live in the dirt. Sometimes they come up to the surface after it rains. Earthworms can even re-grow body parts if they are cut off!

1.   What is the main idea of this passage?

   A.   Earthworms are slimy and have no legs.
   B.   Earthworms like to eat grass.
   C.   Earthworms can re-grow body parts.
   D.   Earthworms are really neat animals.

If you're not sure about the answer, ask yourself some questions.

What is the passage about?

The passage is about earthworms and their many qualities.

Does the title give a hint?

Yes, the title says the passage is about earthworms.

The main idea is "Earthworms are really neat." This is the "big idea" of the passage. The first sentence tells us the main idea. The rest of the sentences tell us *why* earthworms are so neat. These are called **supporting details**. The correct answer is **D**. Great job! Now, try some on your own.

Play Time

Dolphins love to play. They play-fight with other dolphins. They even play with seabirds and turtles. Dolphins like to ride waves. They often "surf" beside boats. They like to jump above the water and do twists and turns, too!

2. What is the main idea of this passage?
    A. Playing is fun.
    B. Dolphins play with other dolphins.
    C. Dolphins like to ride waves.
    D. Dolphins love to play.

Dangerous Pets

Alligators are dangerous, so they don't make good pets. Some people buy baby alligators and try to keep them as pets. Alligators grow fast. Their teeth get very sharp. They can hurt their owners and ruin a house. It is not a good idea to have an alligator as a pet.

3. What is the main idea of this passage?
    A. All pets are dangerous.
    B. Alligators are dangerous pets.
    C. Alligators grow quickly, and their teeth get very sharp.
    D. Some people buy baby alligators and keep them as pets.

Camping

I like to go camping with my family in the summer. We like to swim and hike. Sometimes we get a boat and go fishing. At night, we have a camp fire. We roast marshmallows and hot dogs. Sometimes my dad tells scary stories. Camping is a good time!

4. What is the main idea of this passage?
   - A. Swimming and hiking are fun.
   - B. Fishing is easy.
   - C. Camping is fun.
   - D. Roasting hot dogs is scary.

SUPPORTING DETAILS—THE LITTLE THINGS

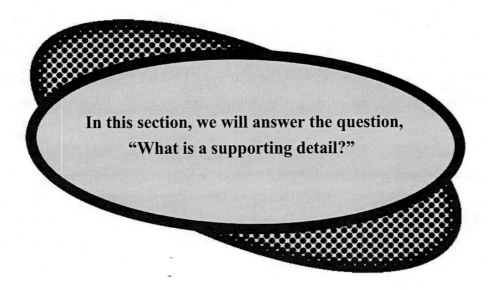

In this section, we will answer the question, "What is a supporting detail?"

Supporting details tell things about the main idea. They are smaller ideas that hold up the main idea. Think about a passage being like a table. The top of the table is the main idea. The details are the legs that hold up the table. They are facts, reasons, and examples that support the main idea. Supporting details make the main idea stronger.

Main Idea and Supporting Details

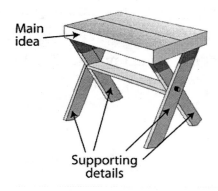

What if your friends said, "We had the best time at Sam's house this weekend!" You would want to know why they had such a good time. The things they did at Sam's house are the supporting details. Read the example below. The supporting details are underlined.

> "We had the best time at Sam's house this weekend! We played video games and jumped on the trampoline. Sam's mom made us ice cream sundaes. Later, we went to the movies."

The main idea is, "We had the best time at Sam's house." All of the other sentences are supporting details. They explain why Sam's house was so much fun.

Practice 2: Supporting Details

ELA3R3-j

Read the passages below. Underline the supporting details in the passage. The first one has been done for you.

Chapter 1

Niagara Falls

1.   Niagara Falls is a beautiful place to visit. It is partly in New York and partly in Canada. There are three waterfalls at Niagara Falls. They are all very big! The biggest one is over 184 feet high.

Let's see how you did. Here is the answer: <u>It is partly in New York and partly in Canada. There are three waterfalls at Niagara Falls. They are all very big! The biggest one is over 184 feet high.</u>

The main idea of the passage is, "Niagara Falls is a beautiful place to visit." The other sentences are all supporting details. They make the main idea stronger. I bet you did great! Try a few more on your own.

Georgia Animals

2.   I like to visit the mountains in North Georgia. Many kinds of animals live in the North Georgia Mountains. Lots of deer live there. There are also raccoons, skunks, and opossums. You have to be careful when you walk around because there are snakes. Many kinds of fish live in the lakes and rivers. In some places, there are bears. There are many birds everywhere. There are so many animals to see.

Sarah Sue's Zoo

3.   Sarah Sue had so many pets, her house looked like a zoo. She had a mouse, a chicken, a pig, a bird, a gerbil, a cat, and a dog. Sometimes the cat would try to eat the mouse or the bird. Sometimes the dog would chase the cat. And sometimes the pig would chase the chicken!

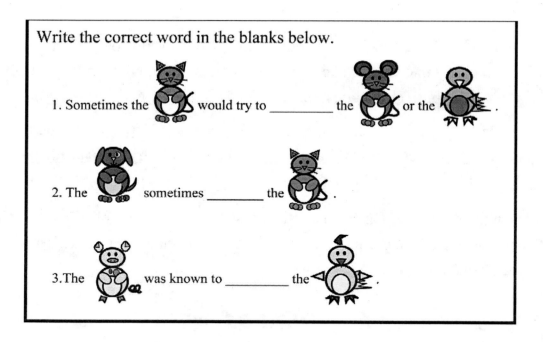

Write the correct word in the blanks below.

1. Sometimes the [cat] would try to _____ the [mouse] or the [bird] .

2. The [dog] sometimes _____ the [cat] .

3. The [pig] was known to _____ the [bird] .

Lincoln Memorial

4. The Lincoln Memorial is an exciting place to visit. It has big columns, 36 of them, in the front. The columns are so big, five adults holding hands cannot reach around one of them. Inside the memorial, there is a 19-foot tall statue of President Lincoln.

CHAPTER 1 SUMMARY

In this chapter, you learned about main ideas and supporting details.

Main idea—what the passage is about. It is the "big idea" of the passage.

Supporting details—the facts, reasons, and examples that explain the main idea.

Don't Forget!

LET'S REVIEW

ELA3R3-j

Here is some more practice with all that you learned in this chapter. Read the following passages. Then answer the questions about them.

Tornado!

Tornadoes are the most dangerous storms on earth! If you ever see a big black cloud with a cone shape at the bottom, look out! It could be a tornado!

When someone has seen a tornado, the weather service puts out a tornado warning. If you hear a warning, a tornado may be near you. The most important thing to do is **TAKE SHELTER** when a tornado is nearby. If you're outside, get inside your house. Go to the basement if you have one. If there isn't a basement, go to a closet on an inside wall, or a bathroom, or a hallway on the lowest level of your house. Stay away from windows.

Tornadoes are scary and dangerous. But, you can be safe during a tornado if you follow these steps.

1. This passage is MAINLY about

   A. how to chase tornadoes safely.
   B. how to stop a tornado.
   C. how to write a story about tornadoes.
   D. how to stay safe if a there is a tornado warning.

2. All of these are supporting details, EXCEPT
    A. Tornadoes are the most dangerous storms on earth!
    B. Stay away from windows.
    C. If you're outside, get inside your house.
    D. Go to the basement if you have one.

Smart and Clean Pigs?

Many people think pigs are dirty or stupid. But, pigs are really very clean and smart. They are even smarter and cleaner than dogs and cats! That's why many people own them as pets.

3. What is the MAIN idea of this passage?
    A. Dogs and cats are smarter than pigs.
    B. Some people don't like pigs.
    C. Many people keep pigs as pets.
    D. Pigs are clean and smart.

4. Which of these is another supporting detail that could be added?
    A. Pigs enjoy taking baths and are easy to train.
    B. Pigs do not like being clean.
    C. Pigs make bad pets.
    D. Pigs are hard to train and not very bright.

Riding a Bike

Riding a bike for the first time can be a little scary. First, you have to push the bike to get it moving. Then, you have to sit down and start pedaling. You have to keep your balance and watch where you're going. You might fall down a few times so remember to always wear a helmet.

5. What is the MAIN idea of this passage?

    A. Riding a bike is dangerous.

    B. Riding a bike is easy.

    C. Riding a bike for the first time can be a little scary.

    D. Safety is the most important thing to remember when riding a bike.

6. Which of these is NOT one of the supporting details in this passage?

    A. push the bike

    B. sit down and start pedaling

    C. inflate the tires

    D. watch where you're going

The Beach

    There are lots of neat things to do at the beach. You can swim or make a sandcastle. You can also look for neat shells or dig for clams. You can play volleyball too.

7. What is the MAIN idea of this passage?

    A. You can swim or make sandcastles at the beach.

    B. You can play volleyball at the beach.

    C. You can look for shells at the beach.

    D. There are lots of neat things to do at the beach.

8. Which of these is another supporting detail that could be added to the passage?

    A. You can have a picnic at the beach.

    B. The beach offers something for everyone to do.

    C. The beach is hard to find.

    D. The beach is dirty and polluted.

Main Idea and Supporting Details

I like to help my parents with chores at home. I help sweep the floors and wipe down the counters. I put away my toys. Sometimes I even help fold the laundry. When I'm done, I get to go outside and play. And, every Friday, I get $5.00 for helping them with the chores. That's the best part!

9. What is the MAIN idea of this passage?
   A. It's fun to play outside.
   B. Helping your parents with chores is boring.
   C. Helping with chores can be fun and rewarding.
   D. Folding laundry is hard.

10. The author helps her parents by
   A. playing outside.
   B. paying her parents $5.00 every week.
   C. watching television and eating junk food.
   D. sweeping, wiping counters, picking up toys, and folding laundry.

Chapter 2
Summarizing, Predicting, & Inferring

This Chapter covers Georgia standards

ELA3R3-b	Makes predictions from text content.
ELA3R3-f	Makes judgments and inferences about setting, characters, and events and supports them with evidence from the text.
ELA3R3-g	Summarizes text content.
ELA3R3-j	Identifies and infers main idea and supporting details.
ELA3R3-m	Recalls explicit facts and infers implicit facts.

When you take the CRCT in reading, you will see questions that ask how well you understand a passage. These questions will ask how well you can figure out what's going on in a passage. In this chapter, we'll talk about how to:

- **summarize** what you read
- **predict** what might happen next
- **infer** ideas about characters and events that are not written

SUMMARIZING

Summarizing a passage means putting it in your own words.

Summarizing, Predicting, & Inferring

A **summary** is a brief way to tell what you've read in a passage or story. When you summarize, you retell it in your own words. A summary is usually very short. It gives the main idea and leaves out the little details. A good summary gives readers the main idea of a passage in very few words.

> **Hint: You read about main idea in chapter 1.**
> **Review that chapter if you need to.**

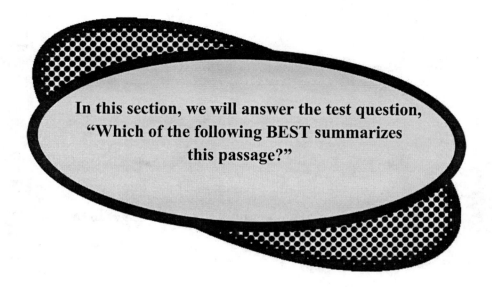

In this section, we will answer the test question, "Which of the following BEST summarizes this passage?"

For example, let's say you have just finished reading the story of "Goldilocks and the Three Bears."

A friend asks you what the story is about. Here is a summary you might give of the story:

"Goldilocks" is about a little girl and three bears. The little girl goes to the bears' house. The bears are not there. She eats their food and sleeps in their beds. The bears come home and find her. Goldilocks runs away.

Chapter 2

Practice 1: Summarizing a Passage

ELA3R3-g, m

The Cat and the Birds

A fable by Aesop

A Cat heard that the Birds in a certain house were feeling sick. He dressed himself up as a doctor. They would not see he was a cat, and he could eat them. He walked with a cane and had a doctor's bag full of things a doctor carries. He went to call on them. He knocked at the door and asked how they were. The Cat said that, if they were ill, he would be happy to help and cure them. They replied, "We are all very well. And we will stay well if you go away and leave us as we are."

1. Which of the following BEST summarizes this passage?

    A. A cat becomes a doctor and helps some birds feel better.

    B. Some birds are not feeling well. A doctor comes to their door, but they will not let him in. They think he is a cat.

    C. A cat hears about some birds that are sick. He dresses up like a doctor and goes to see them, hoping to trick them. But they know it's a cat and tell him to go away.

    D. A cat heard that the birds in a certain house were feeling sick. He wanted to help them. He was a doctor, so he brought his bag to visit them. But the birds were not smart and did not want to see a doctor.

Summarizing, Predicting, & Inferring

Sir Francis Drake

 Francis Drake was a famous English explorer. He sailed the seas to find new ways to get places. He lived in the late 1500s. Drake was the second explorer ever to circumnavigate the globe. That means he went around the whole world in a ship. The first person to do that was Ferdinand Magellan, about 50 years earlier. In Drake's time, England and Spain were enemies. So, the Queen of England asked Drake to help beat the Spanish. Drake made a job out of bothering Spanish ships at sea. He stole from them when he could. In this way, he was also a pirate. Drake spent much of his life at sea.

2. Which line from the passage BEST tells what the whole passage is about?
   A. Francis Drake was a famous English explorer.
   B. He lived in the late 1500s.
   C. In this way, he was also a pirate.
   D. Drake spent much of his life at sea.

3. What is the BEST way to summarize the passage?
   A. Sir Francis Drake spent most of his time on a ship. He sailed around the whole world. He also knew the Queen of England.
   B. Sir Francis Drake was the second person to go around the world in a ship. The first was Magellan. He went around the whole world a long time before Drake did.
   C. Sir Francis Drake was an English explorer in the 1500s. He found new sea routes. He even sailed around the whole world. He also was a pirate because he stole from the ships of England's enemy, Spain.
   D. Sir Francis Drake was from England. The Queen of England asked him to beat the Spanish, who were enemies of the English. He did that, and she probably rewarded him. Maybe he got a new ship for doing a good job.

ACTIVITY: SUMMARIZING

A. Think of the story "The Three Little Pigs." Try to summarize the story. Remember to put it in your own words and to include the main ideas in the story.

B. Think of your favorite stories. Try to summarize one of these stories. Include the main ideas from the story and try to keep it as short as possible.

MAKING PREDICTIONS

A **prediction** is what you think will happen next in a passage or story. You guess what will happen based on what has already happened. It also helps to think about what you know will most likely happen.

You make predictions every day. For example, you predict the weather. If you see dark clouds in the sky, what is most likely to happen? It will probably rain. You have just predicted the weather!

You can make predictions just like this when you read. As you read, use what you already know and the clues in the passage to decide what might happen next. When you read a detective story you make a prediction when you say, "I think this guy did it!"

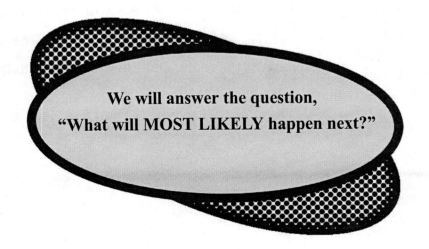

We will answer the question,
"What will MOST LIKELY happen next?"

Summarizing, Predicting, & Inferring

Practice 2:   Making Predictions

ELA3R3-b, m

Read the passages and answer the questions.

The Burger

 Molly sat down at the table with a big, juicy hamburger. She took off the bun and placed a square of orange cheese on the burger. She watched the cheese slowly melt. She put a few pickle slices on top of the cheese. Placing the bun back on the burger, Molly smiled with satisfaction.

"Woof!" Molly's yellow Labrador, Lucy, sat at her side. Lucy cocked her head and twitched her nose. She looked at Molly with eyes that seemed to say, "I want a bite!" Molly smiled. "No, Lucy, you can't have this burger. You have plenty of food in your bowl." Lucy whined softly and stared at the burger. Just then, the phone rang in the other room. Molly jumped up and left the room to answer it. The burger sat on the table, with only a very hungry Lucy to watch over it.

1.   What will Lucy MOST LIKELY do next?

A.   She will eat the burger.   C.   She will go in the other room.

B.   She will take a nap.   D.   She will go eat her dog food.

Did you choose **A**? You're right! We can predict that Lucy will eat the burger because of clues in the passage. Lucy barks, whines, and stares at the burger. Molly tells Lucy that the burger is not for her. Then, Molly leaves the room, and Lucy is alone with the burger. These are clues that let us know that Lucy will probably try to eat the burger, now that she has the chance. Now try some on your own.

Chapter 2

High Dive

I looked down. The pool looked so far away. I was on the high diving board. My toes were on the edge. My friends laughed and splashed below me. "Jump!" they yelled. "Come on, Zack! It's fun!" they laughed. I was the only one who hadn't jumped in yet. I had to do it. I took a big breath and plugged my nose.

2. Based on the passage, what will MOST LIKELY happen next?
   A. Zack will start singing.
   B. Zack will tell a joke.
   C. Zack will take driving lessons.
   D. Zack will jump into the pool.

Winter Snow

Matt and Armando put on their boots, coats, hats, and gloves. They went out into the snow and began making three large balls out of the snow. They stacked them on top of each other. Then, they looked around for two sticks.

3. Can you predict what Matt and Armando are making out of the snow?
   A. Matt and Armando are making a snow fort.
   B. Matt and Armando are making a snowman.
   C. Matt and Armando are making a sled.
   D. Matt and Armando are making a birdhouse.

4. What will the two sticks MOST LIKELY be used for?
   A. the snowman's eyes
   B. the snowman's belly
   C. the snowman's arms
   D. the snowman's teeth

The Moving Egg

One of the eggs in the nest began to move. It wobbled a little to the left and the right. Then, a small crack appeared in the shell. The mother bird sat on the edge of the nest, watching patiently.

5. Based on the passage, what will MOST LIKELY happen next?
   A. The egg will disappear.
   B. The egg will fall and break.
   C. A baby bird will come out of the egg.
   D. The crack in the shell will fix itself.

INFERENCES—MAKING A CONNECTION

When you make an **inference**, you make a connection between what is said and what is not said in a story. Some authors may not tell you everything that happens in a passage. Instead they give you clues that let you know what is happening. Like a detective, you have to connect the clues to solve the case! But, don't worry. This detective work is easy. For instance, look at the passage below.

The Ringmaster came out first. He wore a black hat and a bright red jacket. He held a microphone and said, "Welcome to the Greatest Show on Earth!" Then came elephants and monkeys who did tricks that made us laugh. Next, we saw people flying though the air on a trapeze!

Did you guess this passage is about the circus? You guessed right! The author does not tell us this. So how did you get the answer right? You looked at the clues to figure out what the passage is about. You made an inference!

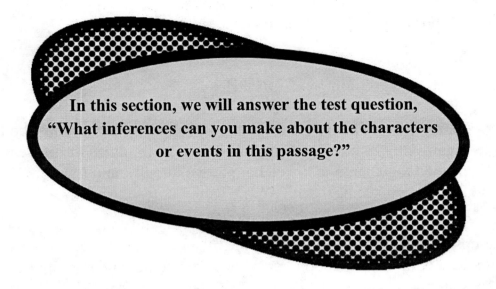

In this section, we will answer the test question, "What inferences can you make about the characters or events in this passage?"

Practice 3: Making Inferences

ELA3R3-b, f, j

Read the passages and answer the questions.

I sat in the waiting room of the doctor's office. It was time for my yearly flu shot. As I waited, I could feel my heart beating quickly. My skin felt cold and I had butterflies in my stomach. I picked up a magazine, but I didn't really read anything. I just flipped through the pages and then picked up another one. I kept looking at the clock, wishing that time would go by faster so I could get it over with. It felt like I had been there for hours. "If only I could fast-forward to this afternoon," I thought.

1. What inference can you make about the author?

    A. The author likes reading magazines.

    B. The author is nervous about getting a flu shot.

    C. The author is very sick and wants to go home.

    D. The author likes visiting doctor's offices.

My Friend

When I woke up, my cat was curled up next to me, her furry body snuggled against my legs. We got out of bed. My cat followed me to the bathroom. We washed together. She licked her paws and belly, and I washed my face and brushed my teeth.

Then, we went to the kitchen. I had cereal, and she had hard, brown little lumps that came in a big bag with the picture of another cat on it. After we ate, we got dressed. I put on her favorite red collar, and she played with the laces on my shoes.

Finally, I said, "Goodbye" and petted her head. I walked out the door and down the driveway to catch the bus to school. I looked back. My cat was at the window, looking back at me.

2. What inference can you make about the author?

    A. The author is kind and gentle to her cat.

    B. The author is a mean and selfish person.

    C. The author doesn't like her cat.

    D. The author is very silly.

3. What can you infer about the cat?

    A. The cat hates to get up early.

    B. The cat will only eat what the author eats.

    C. The cat likes being with its owner.

    D. The cat wishes it could play with other cats.

Chapter 2

In Search of Candy

Noah could barely see. He felt around on the sticky floor for his box of chocolate candy. He put aside his drink and his large tub of popcorn. He bumped his head on the seat in front of him. "Sorry," he mumbled to the person sitting there. He felt around behind his seat. He wanted to find his candy before the previews started.

4. Based on the passage, we can infer that Noah is in
    A. a closet
    B. a movie theatre
    C. his bedroom
    D. at school

CHAPTER 2 SUMMARY

Summarizing—summarizing a passage is briefly telling about what you've read. A summary is a short retelling of a story or passage in your words.

Predicting—when you predict, you tell you think will happen next. You guess what will happen in a story based on what has already happened and on what you know.

Inferring—inferring is making a connection between what's said and not said in a story. The author leaves out information about the story. The details let you know what is missing.

LET'S REVIEW

ELA3R3-b, g, j, m

Read the passages, and answer the questions that follow each one.

I stepped up to the plate and dug my cleat into the dirt. I tapped the home plate three times with my bat for good luck. Bringing the bat into position, I eyed the pitcher and he eyed me. He pitched. Keeping my eye on the ball the best I could, I swung with all my might. In a flash, I heard a sound that was music to my ears: "crack!"

1. Based on the passage, we can infer that the author has
    A. just hit the ball with the bat.
    B. just been hit by the ball.
    C. returned to the dugout.
    D. broken his bat.

2. What inference can we make about the author at the end of the passage?
    A. He is disappointed.
    B. He is angry.
    C. He hears music.
    D. He is happy.

3. What will the boy MOST LIKELY do next?
    A. He will cry.
    B. He will run to first base.
    C. He will hit another ball.
    D. He will go back and sit on the bench.

4. What would be the best title for this passage?
    A. How Baseball Got Started
    B. The Advantages of Wearing Glasses
    C. The Day I Hit a Home Run
    D. Having Fun with Friends at School

Michael waited in the long line with his friends, Tim and Shane. They ate their cotton candy while they waited for their turn to ride on the ferris wheel. This would be the second ride they rode. The first was the bumper cars. Michael loved the bumper cars. He wanted to ride them again. But, his friends wanted to ride the ferris wheel. Michael's tummy felt a little sick. He looked up at how high the ferris wheel went. He was scared of heights. He didn't want his friends to know. They would think he was a chicken. So, he waited in line and tried to think about something else. He was glad the line was long.

5. We can infer this passage is taking place at
   A. a school.
   B. the bus stop.
   C. a carnival.
   D. Michael's house.

6. What will Michael MOST LIKELY do next?
   A. He will yell at his friends.
   B. He will tell his friends he's scared.
   C. He will run to his mother and go home.
   D. He will ride the ferris wheel.

7. How would you BEST summarize this passage?
   A. A boy and his friends are waiting to ride a ferris wheel. He doesn't want to tell them he's scared of heights and would rather ride the bumper cars again.
   B. Three boys are eating cotton candy and getting sick to their stomachs. They will probably all get sick as they ride the ferris wheel.
   C. Rides are fun. Some people like scary rides like the ferris wheel and the roller coasters. Other people like to stay on the ground with rides like bumper cars.
   D. A boy is thinking about riding bumper cars. He likes the bumper cars best, but his friends want to ride the ferris wheel.

Chapter 3
Making Judgments & Drawing Conclusions

ELA3R3-f	Makes judgments and inferences about setting, characters, and events and supports them with evidence from the text.
ELA3R3-l	Identifies and infers cause-and-effect relationships and draws conclusions.

JUDGMENTS—WHAT DO YOU THINK?

A **judgment** is what you think about a passage. It is your opinion about the characters, events, and the story itself. Did you like the story? What did you think of the people in it? Were there mean characters or nice ones? Did the main character do the right thing? Were there any events that made you happy or sad? The answers to these questions are your judgments about these things.

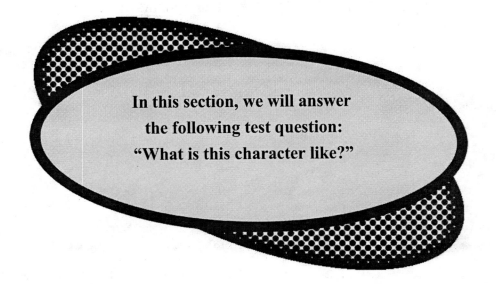

In this section, we will answer
the following test question:
"What is this character like?"

Making Judgments & Drawing Conclusions

For example, read this passage:

Rainy Day Blues

Kelly looked out her bedroom window and frowned. It had been raining for two days. She thought it might stop today. But, lightning lit up the dark sky. And thunder rolled in the distance. She sat on her bed and started to cry. Her pool party would have to be canceled.

What kind of judgment can you make about Kelly? Do you think she seems happy or sad? Kelly seems sad. She's frowning and crying, and her pool party has to be canceled because of the rain. This is a judgment about Kelly—she is sad.

What kind of judgment did you make about the whole story? Were you upset that the rain was keeping Kelly from having her party? Did you think it was unfair? Or did you think Kelly should just stop crying and do something fun indoors?

In the practice that comes next, you can try making judgments on your own.

Practice 1: Making Judgments

ELA3R3-f

Read this story. Then answer the questions that follow.

The Selfish Giant

by Oscar Wilde

Every afternoon, as they were coming from school, the children used to go and play in the Giant's garden.

It was a large lovely garden, with soft green grass. Here and there over the grass stood beautiful flowers like stars, and there were twelve peach-trees that in the spring-time broke out into delicate blossoms of pink and pearl, and in the autumn bore rich fruit. The birds sat on the trees and sang so sweetly that the children used to stop their games in order to listen to them. "How happy we are here!" they cried to each other.

One day the Giant came back. He had been to visit his friend the Cornish ogre, and had stayed with him for seven years. After the seven years were over he had said all that he had to say, for his conversation was limited, and he determined to return to his own castle. When he arrived he saw the children playing in the garden.

"What are you doing here?" he cried in a very gruff voice, and the children ran away.

"My own garden is my own garden," said the Giant; "any one can understand that, and I will allow nobody to play in it but myself." So he built a high wall all round it, and put up a notice-board.

TRESPASSERS WILL BE PROSECUTED

He was a very selfish Giant.

The poor children had now nowhere to play. They tried to play on the road, but the road was very dusty and full of hard stones, and they did not like it. They used to wander round the high wall when their lessons were over, and talk about the beautiful garden inside. "How happy we were there," they said to each other

1. .What judgment can you make about the giant in this story?

   A.   He is a very likable character.

   B.   He is someone you want to be friends with.

   C.   He is sad because he had to end his vacation.

   D.   He is mean and not someone you want to be around.

2. What judgment can you make about how the giant feels?

   A.   The giant loves little children.   C.   The giant loves his garden.

   B.   The giant hates the Cornish orge.   D.   The giant doesn't like to be alone.

3. What judgment can you make about the garden?
   A. The garden is filled with fruit trees.
   C. The garden is full of animals.
   B. The garden is very beautiful.
   D. The garden is always sunny.

4. What judgment can you make about the children?
   A. They don't really care about playing in the giant's garden.
   B. They are very mean children who trespass on other people's gardens.
   C. They are very sad because they can't play in the garden anymore.
   D. They like playing in the road because the giant isn't there.

5. Why do you think the giant was so upset about the children being in his garden?
   A. They were playing in the garden without the giant's permission.
   B. They did not invite the giant to play along with them.
   C. They ripped up the flowers and made a big mess.
   D. They did not know how to care for the garden.

DRAWING CONCLUSIONS—MAKE A STATEMENT

When you draw a **conclusion**, you use the clues in a passage to make a statement about a character or event. You reach a conclusion when you put together all the clues. Like a detective, you conclude that something is most likely true.

Chapter 3

You can draw conclusions by looking at how characters act and what they say. You can also draw conclusions by looking at the setting and the events that happen in a story. Be sure to look at all the details in a passage to see what you can conclude.

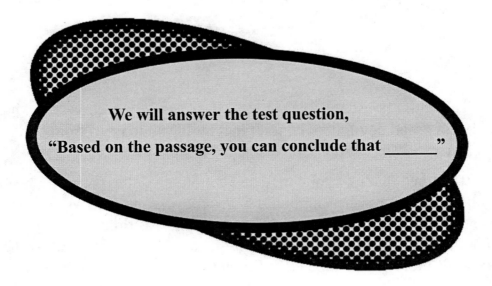

We will answer the test question,

"Based on the passage, you can conclude that _____"

Conclusions are a bit like inferences (guesses about what the author has not told you). If you have not read it already, be sure to read about inferences in **chapter 6**.

As you may know, the word *conclusion* can also mean *ending*. So, a conclusion is a bigger fact or result than small inferences you make along the way. A conclusion is something you can be pretty sure about. You make a conclusion based on the facts in the passage and on other inferences you made

Making Judgments & Drawing Conclusions

For example, read this passage from a mystery story.

The entire household was upset. Mr. Nelson's priceless statue had been stolen in broad daylight! The thief had hit the watchman from behind, so no one saw who did it.

It seemed that everyone here had a motive. Stella, the maid, needed money urgently for her mother to have an operation, and Mr. Nelson did not want to lend it to her. Tom, Mr. Nelson's son, was tired of being told what to do and could not wait to inherit all of his father's money. And Nellie, Mr. Nelson's niece, was jealous that this side of the family had all the riches.

Now, they were all gathered in the study, with Detective Ross asking them questions. "Where were you when this happened, Stella?" he started.

"In the guest room, helping Nellie make the bed," replied Stella.

"Ah, so you two were together," the detective observed. "Tom, what about you?"

"I…uh…I was in the garage." Tom looked around. "I had forgotten something in the car." Detective Ross noticed sweat on his brow.

"But I had the car with me," Mr. Nelson interrupted. Everyone stared at Tom.

"It was a gift for you, Dad," Tom said. "I didn't want you to find it, but you took the car before I could get it out."

© Copyright American Book Company. DO NOT DUPLICATE. 1-888-264-5877.

Chapter 3

Based on this short piece of the story, you can make some inferences and draw some conclusions:

One clue you see is that Tom fumbles when he talks. He is also sweating. You might infer that he had been running. From both clues, you could **conclude** that Tom is nervous.

The maid, Stella, says she was with Nellie when the crime happened. Nellie has not said anything. You can infer that if she does not say Stella is lying, Nellie really was in the same room. If that's true, then Tom is the only person who could have stolen the statue. If you believe Stella, then you can **conclude** that Tom is the thief.

At the end, Tom says that what he was really hiding is a gift for Mr. Nelson. Could this be true? If it is, then you can infer that Stella was lying. In any case, you can **conclude** that someone in this room is lying!

Now, see how you do drawing some conclusions on your own.

Practice 2: Drawing Conclusions

ELA3R3-f

Read the passages and answer the questions.

Making Judgments & Drawing Conclusions

In the Spotlight

Cynthia had practiced for weeks. Her dance teacher, Mrs. Sims, said she was ready. Cynthia heard the music start, and her heart started racing. The lights were hot and bright. She started to move, kicking her leg and turning in circles. Her pink tutu twirled with her. She hoped she wouldn't fall. Everyone was watching her. She swallowed hard and tried to pretend she was alone.

1. What can you conclude about Cynthia based on the passage?

    A. Cynthia is nervous.   C. Cynthia is funny.

    B. Cynthia is angry.   D. Cynthia is smart.

2. Based on the passage, you can conclude that Cynthia is
    A. in a spelling bee.   C. in a soccer game.

    B. in a dance recital.   D. in a gym class.

Coal Mining

Imagine a dark cave hundreds of feet under the ground. The cave is so dark you can barely see. The cave is so cold you shiver. A rat runs past you. The sound of axes and crumbling rock is all around. Imagine this is where you work every day. If you lived before 1840, you might have. Children often worked in caves like this. They were called coal mines. Children would work in these mines from sunrise to sunset. Some days they wouldn't even see the sun.

3. Based on this passage, you can conclude that

    A. children who worked in coal mines had hard lives.

    B. children who worked in coal mines liked to work.

    C. children who worked in coal mines were lazy.

    D. children who worked in coal mines had a lot of fun.

4. What can you conclude about coal mines?
    A. Coal mines are bright and warm.
    B. Coal mines are like big open fields.
    C. Coal mines are scary and dangerous places.
    D. Coal mines are exciting and fun places to work in.

CHAPTER 3 SUMMARY

Judgment—what you think about a passage. It is your opinion about the characters, events, and the story itself.

Conclusion—putting information together to make a statement about a character or event in a passage. You can draw conclusions based on how characters act or what they say, how characters interact, and the setting of a passage.

LET'S REVIEW

ELA3R3-f, 1

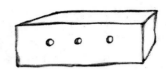

Melissa really wanted a puppy. Most of her friends had a dog. She would play with her friends' dogs when she went to their houses. She asked her parents if she could have a puppy. But, every time she asked her parents said the same thing. They'd say, "A puppy is a lot of work. You have to feed it and water it and give it baths. A puppy also needs to be trained." Her parents didn't think she would be able to do that much work. But, Melissa knew she could. Each day she started to clean her room and picked up her toys. She also helped her parents with other chores. She knew her parents were happy with her new behavior. She hoped her hard work would pay off. One day, when she came home from school, she heard a whining noise coming from a box in the kitchen. There were holes cut in the top and side of the box. Her parents said, "Open it up." Could this be what she'd been working for?

1. Based on the passage, you can conclude that Melissa

    A. started working hard so her parents will know she could care for a puppy.
    B. likes to play inside big cardboard boxes.
    C. loves to do lots of housework and clean up all the time after other people.
    D. doesn't like to help anyone with anything.

2. Based on the passage, what judgment can you make about Melissa?
    A. Melissa is lazy and doesn't like to work hard for anything.
    B. Melissa is smart but she doesn't like to go to school.
    C. Melissa will work hard for something she wants.
    D. Melissa doesn't know the meaning of hard work.

3. Based on the passage, you can conclude that
    A. Melissa's parents will wait until Christmas to get her a puppy.
    B. Melissa's parents will never get Melissa a puppy.
    C. Melissa decides a puppy is too much work and doesn't want one.
    D. a puppy will be inside the box in the kitchen.

4. Based on the passage, you can conclude that Melissa's parents
    A. want to make sure Melissa is able to take care of a puppy.
    B. do not like dogs around the house at all.
    C. are angry because Melissa is helping them around the house.
    D. do not know how to take care of a puppy.

Excerpt from "Dr. Doolittle" by Hugh Lofting

I had expected to find cages with animals inside them. But there were none to be seen. Instead there were little stone houses all over the garden.

Each house had a window and a door. As we walked, many of these doors opened and animals came running out to us expecting food.

"Do the doors have locks on them?" I asked the Doctor.

"Oh yes," he said, "Every door has a lock. But in my zoo the doors open from the inside, not from the outside. The locks are there so the animals can go and shut themselves in any time they want to get away from other animals or from people who come here. Every animal in this zoo stays here because he likes it, not because he is made to."

"They all look very happy and clean," I said. "Would you mind telling me the names of some of them?"

"Certainly. That funny-looking thing with plates on his back is a South American armadillo. The little guy talking to him is a Canadian woodchuck. They both live in those holes you see at the foot of the wall. The two little beasts doing tricks in the pond are a pair of minks. Which reminds me, I must go and get them some fish from the town before noon today. That animal just stepping out of his house is an antelope, one of the smaller kinds. Now let us move to the other side of those bushes and I will show you some more."

"Have you any lions or tigers?" I asked as we moved on.

"No," said the Doctor. "It wouldn't be possible to keep them here. I wouldn't keep them even if I could. If I had my way, Stubbins, there wouldn't be a single lion or tiger in a cage anywhere in the world. They never take to it. They're never happy. They never settle down. They are always thinking of the big lands they left behind. You can see it in their eyes, dreaming—dreaming always of the great open spaces where they were born; dreaming of the deep, dark jungles where their mothers first taught them how to scent and track the deer. And what are they given in exchange for all this?" asked the Doctor, stopping in his walk and growing all red and angry—"What are they given in exchange for the glory of an African sunrise, the twilight breeze whispering through the palms, the shade of the matted vines, for the cool nights of the desert, for the patter of the waterfall after a hard day's hunt? What, I ask you, are they given in exchange for these? Why, a cage with iron bars; an ugly piece of meat thrust in to them once a day; and a crowd of fools to come and stare at them with open mouths!—No, Stubbins. Lions and tigers, the Big Hunters, should never, never be seen in zoos."

The Doctor seemed to have grown terribly serious—almost sad. But suddenly his manner changed again and he took me by the arm with his same old cheerful smile.

"But we haven't seen the butterfly-houses yet—nor the aquariums. Come along. I am very proud of my butterfly-houses."

. . . "Do butterflies have a language?" I asked.

"Oh I fancy they have," said the Doctor–"and the beetles too. But so far I haven't succeeded in learning much about insect languages. I mean to take it up though."

5. What judgment can you make about the Doctor?
    A.   The Doctor is cruel to animals.
    B.   The Doctor wants to keep all animals in cages.
    C.   The Doctor is kind to animals and has a lot of respect for them.
    D.   The Doctor only likes lions and tigers as pets, but not beetles and butterflies.

6. Based on the passage, you can conclude
    A.   The Doctor doesn't think animals should be locked in cages.
    B.   The Doctor thinks only dangerous animals should be kept in cages.
    C.   The Doctor thinks only little animals should be kept in cages.
    D.   The Doctor thinks only humans should be kept in cages.

7. Based on the passage, you can conclude
    A.   The zoo will only have lions and tigers.
    B.   The animals in the zoo will be locked in cages.
    C.   The zoo will only have minks in it.
    D.   The Doctor's zoo will never have lions and tigers in it.

8. the end of the passage, you can conclude that
    A. the Doctor is trying to learn to talk to tigers and lions.
    B. the Doctor is trying to learn to talk to tropical fish in the sea.
    C. the Doctor is trying to learn to talk to butterflies and beetles.
    D. the Doctor is trying to remember how to talk to human beings.

9. What judgment can you make about the animals in the Doctor's zoo?
    A. They are sad.
    B. They are hungry and thirsty.
    C. They are happy and well-cared for.
    D. They are mad at the Doctor for locking them up.

10. If the Doctor saw a tiger or lion locked up in a zoo, he would probably feel

    A. excited and happy.
    B. scared and fearful.
    C. sad and angry.
    D. tired and sleepy.

Chapter 4
Author's Purpose—Why Write This Stuff Anyway?

This chapter covers Georgia standard

ELA3R3-p	Recognizes the author's purpose.

We all write with a reason or a **purpose**. An author has things to say and a point to make. When you read a passage, ask yourself, "Why did the author write this? What is the reason?"

In this chapter, we will learn about reasons for writing.

We will answer this question,
"What is the author's main reason for writing this passage?"

There are many reasons to write. An author can write to **inform** or **teach**. For example, the textbooks you use in school are written to teach you about math or science or reading. An author can write to **entertain**. Examples of this would be comic books, short stories, or novels like *Junie B. Jones*. An author can also write to **persuade** (convince) a reader to do or not do something. For example, a colorful ad can get you to buy a new toy.

Author's Purpose—Why Write This Stuff Anyway?

Practice 1: Author's Purpose

ELA3R3-p

Read the passages and choose the author's purpose. The first one has been done for you.

Come to Lady Bug's

Lady Bug's is the best store! We have the prettiest flowers and plants! You can get red flowers, yellow flowers, and purple flowers too. If you want your plants to be the prettiest, come to Lady Bug's!

1. What is the author's MAIN reason for writing this passage?

    A. To convince readers to buy their plants and flowers at Lady Bug's.
    B. To entertain readers with funny stories about Lady Bug's.
    C. To teach readers about the many kinds of flowers that there are.
    D. To convince readers that flowers are ugly.

Did you choose A? You're right! Great job! The author is trying to convince readers to come to Lady Bug's to buy flowers and plants. The author is not telling funny stories about flowers. So, choice B can't be the right answer. The author is not teaching readers about flowers. So, choice C is incorrect. The author is not trying to convince readers flowers are ugly. So, choice D is not correct either. The best choice is A.

Now, try a few on your own.

Chapter 4

Having Fun in the Sun

 When the weather is warm, we all like to be outside. If you are playing in the sun, remember some safety tips. Put on sun screen so that you don't get a sunburn. Make sure you wear shoes that are right for what you're doing. If you are running around a lot, socks and tennis shoes are easier on your feet than sandals. Many times, playing outside means getting dirty, so wear old clothes…that way, no one will get upset when you come home with stains on them!

2. What is the MAIN purpose of this passage?

   A. The author's purpose is to entertain.

   B. The author's purpose is to persuade.

   C. The author's purpose is to inform or explain.

   D. The author's purpose is to amuse the reader.

The Problem with Gum

"David," said Mrs. Samson. "What is in your mouth?" I froze. I almost swallowed the five pieces of sour-cherry gum I had just started chewing. The sour part was just getting good. "Nothing," I mumbled around the huge ball in my mouth. My classmates laughed. I pushed the gum to the side of my cheek. "Nothing," I said again, clearer. "I don't think that lump in the side of your cheek is nothing," she replied. "Spit it out now," she commanded. I walked to the trash can and sadly spit it out, where it lay like a shining jewel. I wished I could grab it back up and eat it.

3. What is the MAIN reason the author wrote this passage?

   A. To teach readers gum is bad for your teeth.

   B. To convince readers to chew gum in school.

   C. To teach readers how to blow bubbles.

   D. To entertain or amuse readers with a story.

Author's Purpose—Why Write This Stuff Anyway?

The Spelling Bee

The curtain came up. The lights came on. I was prepared. I had studied every word in the dictionary. "Ellen Blosgow!" the announcer yelled into the microphone. I reached the podium at the center of the stage. I looked at the line of judges, ready to spell my heart out. "Ms. Blosgow," said one of the judges "Spell otorhinolaryngology." My mind went blank.

4. What is the author's purpose for writing this passage?
   A. The author's purpose is to inform.
   B. The author's purpose is to persuade.
   C. The author's purpose is to teach.
   D. The author's purpose is to entertain.

CHAPTER 4 SUMMARY

In this chapter, you learned about why people write different texts.

Author's purpose—the reason why an author writes (whether it's a paragraph, a story, an article, or a whole book). An author writes to entertain, to inform, or teach, or to persuade (convince) people to do or not do something.

Chapter 4

LET'S REVIEW

ELA3R3-p

Lincoln's Life

Abraham Lincoln was born in a log cabin on February 12, 1809. As a young boy, he learned to work very hard. When he was 8, he helped his father build a new log cabin. He did not go to school long because he had to work on the farm. But he loved to read. By the time he was 17, Abe knew he wanted to be a lawyer. He was always fair and honest.

He went on to become our 16th President. He was a great President and achieved many things. One of the most important was helping to end slavery.

1. What is the author's purpose for writing this passage?

   A. To entertain readers with a story about Lincoln.
   B. To convince readers Lincoln didn't accomplish anything.
   C. To persuade readers Lincoln was a horrible President.
   D. To inform or teach readers about Lincoln's life.

The Fastest Animal

What is the fastest animal in the world? Do you know? Many people think it's the cheetah. The cheetah is the fastest on land, but the fastest animal in the world is the Peregrine Falcon. It is one fast bird! The Peregrine Falcon can go as fast as 270

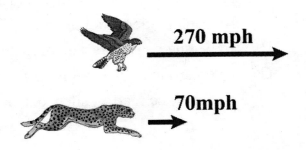

miles per hour. It can reach this speed by diving off of cliffs to catch bugs and other snacks.

2. What is the author's MAIN reason for writing this passage?

   A. To convince readers to buy a Peregrine Falcon.

   B. To entertain readers with stories about how Peregrine Falcons play.

   C. To teach readers about the fastest animal in the world, the Peregrine Falcon.

   D. To inform readers about how deadly and dangerous the Peregrine Falcon is.

No TV?

The next day I arrived at my Grandmother's, heavy suitcase in hand. A few moments later, I found myself seated on Grandma's flowered couch. I picked at the lacy piece of cloth on the arm. The house was quiet, as usual. It was one of the things that bothered me about Grandma's house, the lack of noise.

"Hey Grandma, where's your TV?" I asked, thinking it would give me the noise I needed.

"I don't have one," she replied. Looking at me with laughing eyes. "Never saw the need to get one when I have the radio and books."

"Well, you should think about getting one," I said glumly.

This visit was going to be torture! No TV! No cartoons! How would I make it through two weeks!

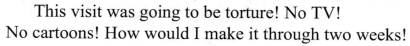

3. What is the author's MAIN reason for writing passage?

   A. To teach readers about good manners.

   B. To persuade readers watching TV is good for them.

   C. To entertain readers with an amusing story.

   D. To convince readers silence is bad.

Chapter 4

Charlie for President

Vote for me on November 16! I'll make sure we have soda for lunch! I'll make sure we get an extra hour of recess every Friday! I'll make school fun again! If you want more fun, don't forget to vote for me on November 16!

4. What is the author's reason for writing this passage?
   A. To persuade readers to vote for him.
   B. To teach readers how to vote.
   C. To inform readers when they need to vote.
   D. To entertain readers with a funny story.

The Best Pet

A dog is a much better pet than a cat. You can play fetch with a dog. You can't do that with a cat. You can also train a dog to do tricks. Cats just stare at you when you want them to do something. Dogs are very loyal too. They will do their best to protect you. If you want a really good pet, get a dog. They are the best kind of pet!

5. What is the author's reason for writing this passage?
   A. To teach readers how to take care of dogs.
   B. To convince readers that cats are better pets than dogs.
   C. To persuade readers that dogs are better pets than cats.
   D. To entertain readers with a funny dog story.

Author's Purpose—Why Write This Stuff Anyway?

New Insta-Veg

Are you tired of eating vegetables? Have you had enough of yucky green stuff? Then tell your mom and dad about Insta-Veg. It's the new pill that gives you a trillion vitamins in one dose. You'll never have to eat broccoli or peas again! Imagine a life free from beans and spinach! Now you can have it with Insta-Veg! Try it now!

6. What is the author's purpose for writing this passage?
   A. To teach readers about good nutrition.
   B. To inform readers about how to stay healthy.
   C. To convince readers that eating vegetables is bad.
   D. To persuade readers to buy Insta-Veg.

The Sock Monster

My mom says, "There is no such thing as monsters." But, I think there is. I think there's a sock monster that lives in my laundry basket. My best friend Jenny thinks so too. Sometimes the monster eats a sock. That's why one sock is missing, even though you know you put two socks in the basket. Also, sometimes the monster just likes to take a little bite of a sock. That's why there's a hole in the toe sometimes. I told my mom about the sock monster. She just laughed and gave me a hug. Then, she said, "I think you might be our little sock monster." I'm not sure what she meant. I don't like to eat socks! But, I'm not scared of the sock monster. He doesn't want to eat me. He just wants to eat my socks.

7. What is the author's purpose for writing this passage?
   A. To convince readers socks are good to eat.
   B. To teach readers how to keep the sock monster away.
   C. To entertain readers with a story about the sock monster.
   D. To persuade readers to buy extra socks for the sock monster.

Chapter 4

The Rainy-Day Fort

Sometimes it is not possible to build a fort outside. Maybe you live in an apartment. Or, maybe you can't go outside because you're grounded. An indoor fort is easy to build. It is also just as fun as an outdoor fort. All you need are some big pillows and a few blankets. Make walls out of the big pillows and some chairs with high backs. Just arrange them into a square shape. Leave a place to crawl in and out. Now, drape the blankets of the top. Next, hop inside and have fun! If the blankets are really old and your parents don't mind, you can cut holes in the blankets to make windows or doors to your fort.

8. What is the author's purpose for writing this passage?
   A. To teach readers how to build a fort inside.
   B. To teach readers how to build a fort outside.
   C. To persuade readers not to build forts inside.
   D. To convince readers forts are dangerous.

The Girl and the Cat

Once upon a time there lived a poor little girl. She was so poor, she had no shoes or a jacket to keep her warm in the winter. She would huddle into a ball and wrap herself in the only blanket she owned, which was full of holes. One night, she heard a strange sound. It was the sound of a cat crying. The little girl went out and found the cat. The cat was thin and cold. The little girl felt sorry for it and brought it back to her house. She shared what little food she had with the cat and wrapped her blanket around it. She petted the cat and talked to it gently. To her great surprise, the cat talked back. The cat said, "I am queen of all cats. Every year I test a person's kindness. You have passed the test, and I will reward you." The cat licked her paw and a necklace appeared. It was a beautiful necklace made of five large white and blue stones. The cat gave it to the little girl. "This necklace is magic. All you have to do is rub each stone three times and make a wish. Whatever you wish will magically appear."

9. What is the author's purpose for writing this passage?
   A. To teach readers how to take care of a cat.
   B. To convince readers cats are bad luck.
   C. To teach readers how to stay warm in winter.
   D. To entertain readers with a story.

Jammin' Joe's Hamburgers

Jammin' Joe's has the best hamburgers in the world! They're big and juicy. We top them with cheese, lettuce, tomato, pickles, ketchup, and mustard. They're the best tasting hamburgers ever! Come to Jammin' Joe's and try the world's BEST hamburger!

10. What is the main reason the author wrote this passage?
    A. To teach readers about how to put toppings on hamburgers.
    B. To entertain readers with a story about making a hamburger.
    C. To convince readers to try a hamburger at Jammin' Joe's.
    D. To persuade readers to never eat hamburgers again.

Chapter 5
Cause & Effect

This chapter covers Georgia standard

ELA3R3-l	Identifies and infers cause- and-effect relationships and draws conclusions.

CAUSE AND EFFECT—ONE THING LEADS TO ANOTHER

When one event causes another to happen, the events have a **cause-and-effect** relationship.

A cause is the reason why something happens. An effect is the result. Look at the example below:

cause: heavy rain

effect: flooding

In this example, heavy rain causes flooding. Heavy rain is the cause. Flooding is the effect.

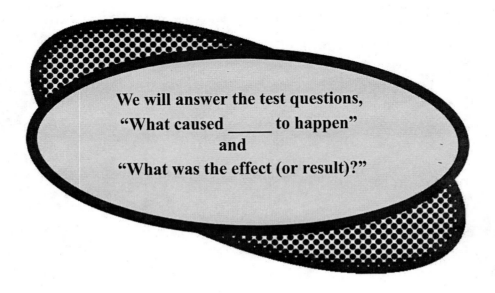

We will answer the test questions,
"What caused _____ to happen"
and
"What was the effect (or result)?"

Cause & Effect

Let's practice.

Practice 1:   Cause and Effect

ELA3R3-1

Read the list of causes below each effect. Choose the correct cause for each effect. Remember the effect is the result. The cause is the reason why the result happened. The first one has been done for you.

1. **Effect:** sleepiness
    Causes:

    A.   too much sleep
    B.   not enough sleep
    C.   not enough milk
    D.   too much yawning

If you picked B, you're right! Not getting enough sleep causes you to be sleepy. Answer A is not the best one because too much sleep doesn't usually make someone sleepy. Answer C is not best because not drinking enough milk shouldn't make you sleepy either. And answer D, yawning, is a sign of sleepiness, but it's not really a cause. The best answer is B. Good work. Try the next ones on your own.

2. **Effect:** The elephant got fat.
    Causes:

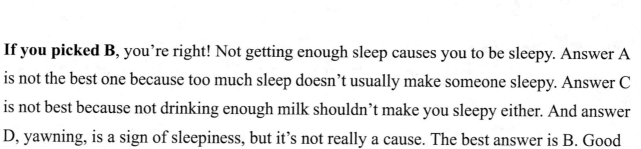

    A.   too much food.
    B.   too much exercise
    C.   not enough sun
    D.   not enough sleep

3. **Effect:** Jim was a great tennis player.

Causes:

    A.   shopped for new tennis clothes

    B.   talked daily on the telephone

    C.   watched many hours of television

    D.   practiced playing tennis every day

4. **Effect:** Sarah was grounded for the weekend.

Causes:

    A.   getting good grades

    B.   taking out the trash

    C.   talking back to parents

    D.   cleaning up her room

Now, let's look at causes. Pick the result that will MOST LIKELY happen.

5. **Cause:** I missed the school bus.

Effect:

    A.   I got to school early.

    B.   I got to school on time.

    C.   I got to school late.

    D.   I ran to the bus stop.

6. **Cause:** Carlos studied very hard for the math test.

Effect:

    A.   Carlos did well on the test.

    B.   Carlos didn't take the test.

    C.   Carlos did poorly on the test.

    D.   Carlos doesn't like math tests.

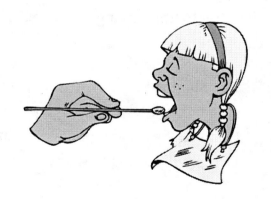

7. **Cause:** Sandra never brushed her teeth.
Effect:

    A.   Sandra had clean teeth.
    B.   Sandra had shiny, white teeth.
    C.   Sandra had a toothbrush.
    D.   Sandra got cavities.

IDENTIFYING CAUSE AND EFFECT IN A PASSAGE

On the CRCT Reading test, you may be asked to tell what caused something in a passage. Or you may be asked to choose the effect of something. This is easy! You answered the questions in the first practice, so you can do this, too. Here are some ways to identify (find) cause and effect relationships.

1. Look for causes and effects by thinking of a timeline. Make a **timeline** of events in a passage (on paper or in your head). Then, you can tell what happened first, next, after that, and last. Now, you can decide which events caused something to happen next.

2. Look for signal words. **Signal words** help show cause-and-effect relationships. Here are some common words that can signal cause and effect:

because	for this reason	this is how	this is why	so
so that	as a result of	if...then	due to	therefore

3. Look for effects that are also causes. Effects can form a chain. That means a cause makes something happen—which is the effect. Then, that effect makes something else happen—so it is the cause of the next effect. This chain can go on for a long time!

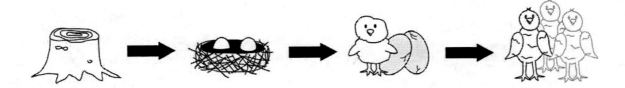

For example, when people cut down trees, birds can't build nests in those trees. When the birds have no place to nest, fewer baby birds hatch. Because fewer babies hatch, the number of birds goes down.

Cause 1: People cut down trees.

Effect 1: Birds can't use those trees for nesting.

This becomes Cause 2.

Effect 2: Fewer babies hatch.

This becomes Cause 3.

Effect 3: The number of birds goes down.

Now, let's try using these ways of finding causes and effects. Read this passage. Then we'll practice.

Cause & Effect

The Golden Spike

In the early 1800s, travel was slow. Some people used the stage coach. It was expensive and took a long time. There were bandits along the way. Others traveled by covered wagon. It was scary. Sometimes they ran out of supplies. As a result, there was just no easy way to go from the East to California. The railroad companies had an idea. They said they would build tracks across America. It would make travel safer and faster. They would call it the Transcontinental Railroad because it went all the way across the continent. Congress gave land for the tracks. Work started on the tracks in 1862.

At first, progress was slow due to the Civil War. But the war ended. More men could work on the railroad, and this is how the tracks grew faster. They would soon meet in the middle. The east and west sides came closer together. New towns sprang up along the tracks. The workers laid tracks in hard winters and across very hot desert. But they finished the railroad.

On May 10, 1869, the two sides of the tracks met at Promontory Summit, Utah. A golden spike was used to nail in the last piece of track. It was made of gold because this was a big event. The spike is a symbol of the nation being joined by the new railroad.

Think about all the events in this passage.

How do they happen?

Which ones cause others?

Now answer this question. Then read the explanation after it.

Chapter 5

Why was the progress slow when they started building the Transcontinental Railroad?

- A. because there were bandits along the way
- B. because there was no land to build on
- C. because it was the time of the Civil War
- D. because hard winters and hot deserts slowed the work

Did you choose answer C? Great job! Did you make a **timeline** of events (on paper or in your head)? If so, it was easy to pick the right answer. Answer A is not right—the passage says that bandits attacked stage coaches *earlier*. Answer B is not right—your timeline tells you that Congress gave land *before* building began. And answer D is not right because the hard winters and hot deserts made the work difficult *later* in the building.

Answer **C** is the best answer. Another reason you know this is because the sentence in the passage uses a **signal word**. The passage says, "At first, progress was slow *due to* the Civil War." The words *due to* mean that something happened because of something else. So, building of the tracks was slow (**effect**) *due to* the Civil War (**cause**).

Did you think about how one thing led to another? For example, look at these possible questions about effects that can also be causes:

Cause 1: People wanted to travel more safely and quickly across America.

Effect 1: Railroad companies decided to build the Transcontinental Railroad. (**becomes Cause 2**)

Cause 2: Railroad companies start building the railroad.

Effect 2: Towns spring up along the tracks.

ACTIVITY: IDENTIFYING CAUSE AND EFFECT IN A PASSAGE

Read the passage "The Golden Spike" again.

A. Make a list of all the signal words you see. Write down what the cause and the effect for each signal word. The first on is done for you.

CAUSE: <u>time, money, bandits</u>
SIGNAL WORD: <u>as a result of</u>
EFFECT: <u>no easy way to go from the East to California</u>

CAUSE: _____
SIGNAL WORD: _____
EFFECT: _____

CAUSE: _____
SIGNAL WORD: _____
EFFECT: _____

CAUSE: _____
SIGNAL WORD: _____
EFFECT: _____

B. Look for the cause-and-effect chains. For example, earlier you read that people wanted to travel more safely and quickly (Cause 1), so the Transcontinental Railroad was started (Effect 1). And because the Transcontinental Railroad was started (Cause 2), towns were built along the tracks (Effect 2). Can you find others?

Cause 1: _____

Effect 1: _____ (becomes Cause 2)

Cause 2: _____

Effect 2: _____

Cause 1: _____

Effect 1: _____ (becomes Cause 2)

Cause 2: _____

Effect 2: _____

Now, try to answer some questions on your own. Do the next practice.

Practice 2:   Identifying Cause and Effect in a Passage

ELA3R3-1

Read the passage below. As you read, think about why the events happen. Then, answer the questions.

Landslides

Sometimes it rains so much that the earth moves! If it rains a lot in a short amount of time, the ground gets soaked. The hard ground turns into soft mud. In very hilly areas, this wet ground can result in a landslide. When this happens, mud starts to flow down a hillside. The landslide moves faster and faster as it goes down the steep hill. It picks up more dirt, mud, and rocks as it moves along. This makes the landslide grow. It is similar to the way a snowball gets bigger when you roll it in the snow. Landslides can cause a lot of damage. People should have an emergency plan ready if they think there might be landslides in their area.

1. What is the MAIN cause of landslides?

A. a hillside

B. heavy rain

C. flat land

D. people

Cause & Effect

2. What happens as a landslide moves down a hill?
    A. It gets bigger.
    B. It slows down.
    C. It stops moving.
    D. It gets soaked.

On the Wind

Jacob held the string tightly and began to run. The kite began to fly. The wind lifted it high in the sky. Jacob kept running. Looking behind him, he watched the kite. He didn't see the group of tall trees he was running toward. The kite dived toward the trees. It got tangled up in the branches. Jacob pulled on the string to get it out of the trees. But all he heard was a cracking sound. Jacob was sad because he knew his new kite was broken. He wouldn't be able to fly it anymore.

3. Why did the kite break?
    A. Jacob was running too fast.
    B. The wind was too strong.
    C. The kite got tangled up in tree branches.
    D. The kite was broken by a bully on the playground.

4. What happened when Jacob pulled on the kite?
    A. He got it out of the trees.
    B. The kite began to fly again.
    C. The kite flew higher.
    D. The kite broke.

5. Why was Jacob sad?
    A. because his kite flew away
    B. because his kite was broken
    C. because the string stung his hand
    D. because he couldn't run faster

CHAPTER 5 SUMMARY

Cause and Effect—when one event causes another to happen, the events have a cause and effect relationship. A cause is the reason why something happens. An effect is the result.

When you need to find causes and effects in a passage:

- Think about the **timeline** of events, so you can figure out what events caused others to happen.
- Look for **signal words**.
- Remember that some effects can become causes of other effects. This is a **cause-and-effect chain**.

LET'S REVIEW

ELA3R3-l

Read the passages. Then, answer the questions that follow.

The Shepherd Boy

A Fable by Aesop

There was once a young Shepherd Boy. He tended his sheep at the foot of a mountain near a dark forest. It was kind of lonely for him all day. So he thought up a plan by which he could get a little company and some fun. He ran down toward the village, calling out "Wolf, wolf!" The villagers came out to meet him, and some of them stopped to talk with him for a long time. This pleased the boy so much that a few days later he tried the same trick. And again, the villagers came to his help. But shortly after this a wolf actually did come out from the forest. The sheep were scared. The boy again cried out "Wolf, wolf!" Nothing happened. He shouted louder: "Wolf, wolf!" But this time, no villagers came out. The boy had fooled them twice before, so they thought he was again doing it again. Nobody came to help him. So the wolf made a good meal of the boy's flock. When the boy complained, the wise man of the village said:

"A liar will not be believed, even when he speaks the truth."

1. When the Shepherd Boy lied, what result did this cause?

   A. The villagers didn't believe what the boy said anymore.

   B. The Wolf ate the boy.

   C. The sheep ran away.

   D. The villagers always believed what the boy said.

2. Why did the Shepherd Boy trick the villagers?

   A. because he was scared   C. because he was lonely

   B. because he was angry   D. because he was happy

Read these sentences. Decide which cause and effect go BEST together.

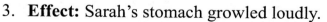

3. **Effect:** Sarah's stomach growled loudly.
Cause:

   A. She missed breakfast.   C. She ate way too much.

   B. She ate too quickly.   D. She is talking to herself.

4. **Effect:** Noah's room was a mess.
Cause:

   A. Noah always cleaned his room.

   B. Noah never cleaned his room.

   C. The invisible man made a mess of Noah's room.

   D. Aliens kidnapped Noah so he could not clean his room.

5.   **Cause:** Maria watered her garden every day.

Effect:

   A.   The garden withered and died.   C.   The garden did not grow well.

   B.   The water flooded Maria's house.   D.   The plants and flowers grew well.

6.   **Cause:** John ran every day.

Effect:

   A.   John was very lazy.   C.   John was good at math.

   B.   John was fit and healthy.   D.   John had new running shoes

The following passage is a retelling of one of Aesop's fables. Read the passage and then answer the questions that follow.

The Fox and the Cat

One hot day, a Fox and a Cat were sitting by a stream. As they cooled themselves with a drink of water, the Fox bragged to the Cat about how clever he was. "As a Fox, I am the cleverest animal of all. I do not fear my enemies because I have a hundred ways to escape them. My bag of tricks is never empty."

The Cat replied, "Well, I guess I only have one way to escape my enemies. But that way has always worked for me." Suddenly, they heard rustling and barking in the woods nearby. It was a pack of hound dogs. They were running straight towards the Cat and the Fox. The Cat quickly ran up a nearby tree and hid herself in the leaves of a high branch. The Cat called to the Fox, "This is my one plan. What is yours?"

The Fox thought of one plan, then another, and yet another. Just as he thought he had settled on a plan, he changed his mind and tried to think of a better plan. The barking grew louder and louder as the dogs approached. They were very close. They were so close that the Fox could see the dogs' tongues hanging out as they panted in the heat. This made him even more frantic. Unfortunately, it was too late for the Fox. The dogs and their hunters trapped the Fox and carried him away. As the Cat looked on from her safe perch, she thought, "It's better to have one safe plan than many plans you are unsure of."

7. Why did the Cat run up the tree?
   A. Because she needed to escape the dogs.
   B. Because she wanted to sleep on a branch.
   C. Because it was a hot day and it was cool in the tree.
   D. Because it was one of the Fox's plans.

8. Why were the Cat and the Fox sitting by the stream?
   A. The stream protected them from their enemies.
   B. It was a hot day and they needed a drink of water.
   C. They were leading the dogs to the stream.
   D. The were trying to escape from the dogs.

9. What caused the Fox to get trapped by the dogs and hunters?
   A. He ran up the tree but they caught him anyway.
   B. He thought that he would not get trapped.
   C. He could not run as fast as the cat could.
   D. He could not pick an escape plan in time.

10. What happened to the Fox as the dogs came closer?
    A. He wasn't worried because he had many plans to choose from.
    B. He quickly thought of an escape plan and ran to safety.
    C. He became more frantic because he was running out of time.
    D. He thought that the dogs would try to get the Cat instead.

Chapter 6
Is It a Fact?

This chapter covers Georgia standards

ELA3R3-d	Distinguishes fact from opinion.
ELA3R3-m	Recalls explicit facts and infers implicit facts.

On the CRCT Reading test, you will be asked to tell the difference between a fact and an opinion. These questions are really easy! Everything you need is in the passage. No guessing! It just takes a little time to think about it.

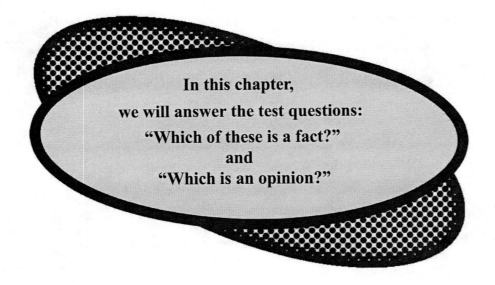

In this chapter,
we will answer the test questions:
"Which of these is a fact?"
and
"Which is an opinion?"

Is It a Fact?

A **fact** is information that is true and can be proven.

Examples:

A praying mantis is a kind of insect.

Earth goes around the sun.

My cat is five years old.

An **opinion** may be true but it cannot be proven. It is usually a person's feelings about something. Words like *I feel*, *I think*, and *in my opinion* are often used in opinions. Sometimes words like *best*, *worst*, *favorite*, *number one*, are also used in opinions.

Examples:

A praying mantis is scary.

Earth is the best planet in the solar system.

My cat is the sweetest and most cuddly cat ever!

To see if something you read is a fact, ask yourself, "Is this true? Can it be proven?" To check to see if it is an opinion, ask yourself, "Is this a feeling or thought?" Now that you know a little more about facts and opinions, let's practice.

Practice 1: Facts and Opinions

ELA3R3-d, m

Read the sentences that follow. Decide if the sentence is a fact or an opinion. The first one has been done for you.

1. My friend's house is the coolest!

☐ Fact
☑ Opinion

Did you choose **opinion**? Correct! This sentence is an opinion. How do we know this? We know it is an opinion because it is how one person feels. Not everyone would agree. It cannot be proven. Try the next ones on your own.

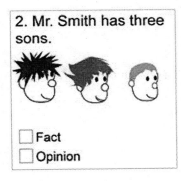

2. Mr. Smith has three sons.

☐ Fact
☐ Opinion

3. Some birds eat worms.

☐ Fact
☐ Opinion

4. Kittens are so cute when they play.

☐ Fact
☐ Opinion

5. Reading is the best way to have fun!

☐ Fact
☐ Opinion

6. Mars is sometimes called the red planet.

☐ Fact
☐ Opinion

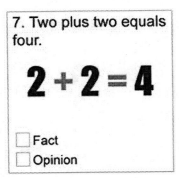

7. Two plus two equals four.

$2 + 2 = 4$

☐ Fact
☐ Opinion

FINDING FACTS IN A PASSAGE—STATED FACTS AND HIDDEN FACTS

Good readers are like detectives. They are able to pick out information in a passage to answer questions. To answer questions about facts and details in a passage, read the passage to find what you need. Some facts will be right there in front of you. These are *stated facts*. Other facts will be *implied*. That means they are not written down, but you can tell they apply.

Remember when you read in chapter 2 about making **inferences**? An **implied fact** is a one that you can infer (guess from what's around it). For example, read this passage:

A fire engine screamed down Elm Street. It rounded the corner at State Street and came to a stop. It was Charlie's house! The firemen rushed in. Smoke came out the back of the house. More firemen attached the hose to the hydrant on the corner and ran toward the house with it.

Now, look at the stated facts and implied facts in this passage:

A fire engine stopped in front of Charlie's' house.
Is this a stated fact or an implied fact?

Did you say it is a **stated fact**? You're right! The passage says that the fire engine rounded the corner and stopped, and then the author says that it was Charlie's house it stopped at.

Smoke came out of the house.
Is this a stated fact or an implied fact?

Did you say **stated fact**? You're right again! The passage says that smoke came out of the back of the house.

Charlie's house is on fire.
Is this a stated fact or an implied fact?

Chapter 6

Did you say **implied fact**? Good job! All the facts in the passage mean that Charlie's house is on fire. But, the author never writes the words, "Charlie's house is on fire." We just know it's true from the clues. This is an implied fact.

To make sure you know all the stated and implied facts, you may have to look at the passage a second time. If it's a long passage with many details, you'll likely need to read it a few times. You do not have to read the whole passage over and over. Just look for what you need to answer the question. Let's practice.

Practice 2: Finding Facts in a Passage

ELA3R3-d, m

Read the passages below. Then answer the questions that follow. The first one has been answered for you.

The Sun

The Sun is a star. I think it's the greatest star in the universe! The Sun is really, really hot. The Sun's average surface temperature is 10,000°F. Compare that to the Earth's average temperature, which is about 60°F. The Sun is also a lot bigger than the Earth. More than one million planets the size of Earth could fit inside of the Sun!

Our Sun gives us light, heat. and energy. Without the Sun, life on Earth would not exist. It would be so cold that no living thing would be able to survive. Our planet would be completely frozen.

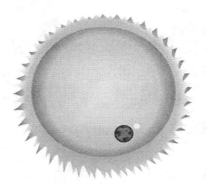

1. What is the average temperature of the Sun?
   A. 20,000° F
   B. 10,000° F
   C. too hot
   D. no one knows

Is It a Fact?

Did you choose answer B? You got it! The answer to this question is in the passage. All you have to do is look back at the passage to find this fact about the Sun. The answer is 10,000° F. Good work! Now try some on your own.

2. Which of the following is a **fact**?
   A. The Sun is the greatest star in the universe.
   B. Learning about the Sun is boring.
   C. The Sun is a star.
   D. The Sun is icy.

3. According to the passage, what does the Sun give us?
   A. sunburns
   B. the ebb and flow of the oceans
   C. 12 hours of light every day
   D. light, heat, and energy

4. How many planets the size of Earth can fit inside the Sun?
   A. about one hundred
   B. more than ten thousand
   C. more than one million
   D. about ten million

5. Which of the following is an **implied fact** of this passage?
   A. The Sun is a very big star.
   B. The Sun is very important for life on Earth.
   C. Without the Sun, life on Earth would not exist.
   D. We get light from the Sun.

CHAPTER 6 SUMMARY

Facts—information that is true and can be proven. To see if something you read is a fact, ask yourself, "Is this true? Can it be proven?"

Don't Forget!

Opinions—may be true but cannot be proven. Opinions are usually a person's feelings about something. To check to see if it is an opinion, ask yourself, "Is this a feeling or belief?" Look for words like *I feel, I think, in my opinion, best, worst, favorite, number one*, etc.

Chapter 6

Finding Facts in a Passage—to answer questions about facts and details in a passage, read the passage to find what you need. You may have to look at the passage a second or a third time. Remember that there are stated facts and implied facts.

Stated Facts—are facts that the author has written. They are right there in front of you.

Implied Facts—these facts are not written, but you can tell they apply. An implied fact is something you can infer (see chapter 2 for more about inferences).

LET'S REVIEW

ELA3R3-d, m

Read the following sentences. Decide whether the sentence is a fact or an opinion.

1. Frog legs are delicious and yummy to eat.
   A. fact   B. opinion

2. London is the capital city of England.
   A. fact   B. opinion

3. Christmas is celebrated on December 25.
   A. fact   B. opinion

4. I think people who live in small towns are friendly.
   A. fact   B. opinion

5. The best part about Thanksgiving is pumpkin pie.
   A. fact   B. opinion

6. Dr. Martin Luther King, Jr., was born in Atlanta, Georgia.
   A. fact   B. opinion

Is It a Fact?

Read the passage below. Decide which statements are facts and which are opinions.

A butterfly's life is really cool. A butterfly begins as a tiny egg on a plant. When the egg hatches, it isn't a baby butterfly. It's a tiny caterpillar! The caterpillar eats a lot of leaves and plants. It grows bigger and bigger. Then its skin starts to harden. The skin forms a shell. Bug doctors call this a "chrysalis." Inside the shell, the caterpillar changes quickly. After some time, a butterfly comes out. The butterfly is wet and its wings are wrinkled. It looks a little funny when it comes out of its shell. It stays still until its wings harden. Then, it flies away. I think butterflies are the coolest bugs!

7. Which of the following sentences from the passage is a fact?
    A.   A butterfly's life is really cool.
    B.   It looks a little funny when it comes out of its shell.
    C.   A butterfly begins as a tiny egg on a plant.
    D.   I think butterflies are the coolest bugs!

8. Which of the following is an opinion?
    A.   The caterpillar eats a lot of leaves and plants.
    B.   Inside the shell, the caterpillar changes quickly.
    C.   The butterfly is wet and its wings are wrinkled.
    D.   I think butterflies are the coolest bugs!

9. Which of the following is an opinion?
    A.   Caterpillars are ugly.
    B.   Caterpillars eat plants.
    C.   Caterpillars form a chrysalis.
    D.   Caterpillars turn into butterflies.

10. Which of the following is a fact?
    A.   Butterflies are the most interesting insects in the world.
    B.   Butterflies are the most disgusting insects in the world.
    C.   Butterflies live in all parts of the world.
    D.   Butterflies don't like living by the ocean.

Chapter 7
Context Clues and Multiple Meanings

This chapter covers Georgia standards

| ELA3R2-b | Uses grade-appropriate words with multiple meanings. |
| ELA3R2-f | Determines the meaning of unknown words on the basis of context. |

On the CRCT reading test, you will see questions about vocabulary (word meaning). You may see words you don't know. Don't worry. You're not alone. There are millions of words out there. No one knows the meaning of all of them.

But, you can figure out the meaning of new words. Even without a dictionary, there are ways to figure out words. In this chapter, you will learn some of those ways.

One of the best ways to figure out the meaning of a new word is to use context clues.

CONTEXT CLUES—THE WORDS AROUND THE WORD

Context means what's around something. When you see a word you do not know, look at the words around it.

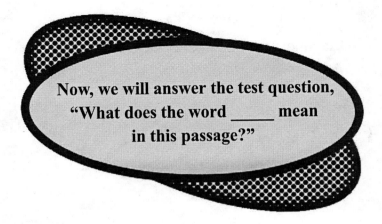

Now, we will answer the test question, "What does the word _____ mean in this passage?"

Context Clues and Multiple Meanings

Context clues give you hints about the meaning of a new word. Context clues come from *the words around* the new word. Look at the example below:

The hike was strenuous.

Look at the word *strenuous*. You may not know what this word means. Looking at it by itself doesn't tell you much about the meaning of the word. It could mean that the hike was fun. Or it could mean that the hike was scary. It could mean almost anything if you don't know the word.

Now, look at the word in context:

We walked a long way. The trail went up a steep hill. The hike was *strenuous*. I had to stop and rest before walking again.

The words around the word *strenuous* are the context clues. Can you figure out what *strenuous* means using context clues? Look at the words around the word to figure it out. The first sentence tells us that the author walked a long way. The second sentence says that the trail was steep, so the author had to walk uphill. The last sentence tells us the author has to stop and rest. Based on these clues, we can guess that the word *strenuous* means **hard** or **difficult**.

When you're not sure what a word means, look at the words around the new word for clues. Now that you know a little more about context clues, let's practice.

Chapter 7

Practice 1: Context Clues

ELA3R2-b, f

Read the sentences below and answer the questions. The first one has been done for you.

I *hesitated* before I jumped off the diving board. The pool below looked so far away. It was a little scary. I had to take a moment to work up the nerve to jump.

1. What does the word *hesitated* mean?
    A. paused
    B. looked
    C. ran
    D. jumped

Did you choose **A**? You're right! The other sentences in the passage give you clues to the meaning. The first and second sentences say the pool was far away and the author is scared. The last sentence says that the author had to take a moment before jumping. With these clues, we can correctly guess that hesitated means to pause. Now try a few on your own.

Bobby was a *tyrant* in school. He always bossed everyone around and made fun of people. Sometimes he would take lunch money from other kids.

2. The word *tyrant* means
    A. nice.
    B. funny.
    C. a bully.
    D. a good student.

After playing soccer all day, Carlos was *exhausted*. All he wanted to do was go home and sleep.

3. *Exhausted* means
    A. a hero.
    B. tired.
    C. excited.
    D. scared.

Context Clues and Multiple Meanings

The thought of eating bugs is *repugnant* to most people. But in some countries eating insects is considered a treat. But most people I know think it's nasty.

4. What does *repugnant* mean?
   A. enjoyable
   B. difficult
   C. gross
   D. old

Did you know that a praying mantis, a big bug, can *rotate* his head in a full circle? He can see in every direction.

5. What does *rotate* mean?
   A. turn
   B. jump
   C. stand
   D. open

There are two *species* of camel. You can tell them apart by the number of humps on their backs. One type of camel has one hump, and the other has two humps.

6. *Species* means
   A. bugs.
   B. cracks.
   C. back.
   D. kinds.

Our *meager* meal was only a few crumbs of bread. Our lunch was not even enough for a mouse.

7. The word *meager* means
   A. first.
   B. large.
   C. delicious.
   D. small.

After riding the roller coaster, Kelly became *nauseous*. Her tummy felt so bad she had to leave the carnival.

8. What does *nauseous* mean?
   A. sick
   B. blind
   C. fat
   D. mad

94

WORDS WITH MULTIPLE MEANINGS—WHAT'S MY MEANING?

Some words have more than one meaning. Sometimes a word can look the same but mean something different in a new context. Remember about **context** from the last section in this chapter?

For instance, the word *bark* has more than one meaning. It could mean a dog's *bark*, or it could mean the *bark* on a tree. Context clues can help you figure out which meaning should be used. Let's put the word *bark* in a sentence: "The woodpecker pecked at the bark." When we look at context clues in this sentence, the meaning becomes clear. It's the hard outside covering of a tree. We can figure out which meaning is right.

Let's practice.

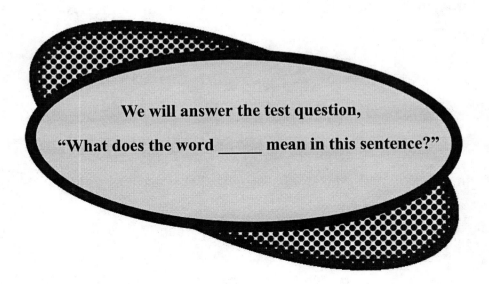

We will answer the test question,

"What does the word _____ mean in this sentence?"

Context Clues and Multiple Meanings

Practice 2:   Words with More Than One Meaning

> ELA3R2-b, f

Look at the list of words below. Choose the right word to correctly complete each sentence. Hint: Each word is used twice. The first one has been done for you.

stick   **star**   **rose**

pet   **can**   **light**

1. If you get glue on your hands, they will _____ together.
   A. stick
   B. star
   C. bat
   D. sink

Which word from the list fits in this sentence? The correct answer is **A**, *stick*. Glue will make your fingers stick together. Now try the rest on your own.

2. My dog chased the _____ when I threw it.
   A. stick
   B. pet
   C. light
   D. sink

3. The brightest _____ in the sky is Sirius.
   A. stick
   B. star
   C. rose
   D. can

4. Elizabeth will _____ in the school play.
   A. stick
   B. star
   C. bat
   D. sink

5. My cat likes it when I _____ her.
   A. star
   B. rose
   C. pet
   D. light

6. You can buy goldfish at a _____ store.
   A. stick
   B. rose

   C. bat
   D. pet

7. My dad opened a _____ of beans.
   A. stick
   B. bat

   C. can
   D. sink

8. "I _____ do it by myself," Ethan said.
   A. star
   B. bat

   C. pet
   D. can

9. It was getting dark so I turned on the _____.
   A. star
   B. bat

   C. light
   D. sink

10. My pet parakeet is as _____ as a feather.
    A. stick
    B. pet

    C. light
    D. sink

11. Sarah gave her mother a beautiful red _____ for her birthday.
    A. stick
    B. rose

    C. can
    D. sink

12. The sun _____ bright and cheery over the horizon.
    A. stick
    B. star

    C. rose
    D. can

CHAPTER 7 SUMMARY

Context clues—the words or sentences around a new word.

Context clues give you hints about the meaning of a new word.

Multiple Meanings—words that have more than one meaning.

LET'S REVIEW

ELA3R2-b, f

Read the sentences below and answer the questions.

> Sarah had a sore throat. Her voice was so soft it was almost *inaudible*. We could barely hear what she was trying to say to us.

1. What does *inaudible* mean?
   - A. annoying
   - B. hard to hear
   - C. talking loudly
   - D. food that is not eatable

> Steven turned *abruptly*. He moved so quickly he almost knocked into the principal.

2. What does the word *abruptly* mean?
   - A. fast and sudden
   - B. slow and clumsy
   - C. quiet and sneaky
   - D. polite and proper

The lake was *tranquil*. Everything was calm and silent.

3. What does the word *tranquil* mean?

A. scary   C. noisy

B. peaceful   D. crazy

Sally was very *gregarious*. She always smiled and talked to everyone. No wonder she was so popular.

4. *Gregarious* means

A. outgoing.   C. scared.

B. sad.   D. stuck-up.

There were several *confections* on the table: There were chocolate chip cookies, three chocolate cakes, and four apple pies.

5. What are *confections*?

A. sweet desserts   C. cakes

B. sandwiches   D. fruit and cheese

Context Clues and Multiple Meanings

Read the sentences below. Choose the answer that has the same meaning as the **bolded word** in the original sentence.

6. Matt held the **bat** tightly as he waited for the pitcher to throw the ball.

   A.   I watched my cat bat at a dragonfly.

   B.   The bat hung upside down in the dark cave.

   C.   Charlie threw down his bat after striking out.

   D.   Matt is as blind as a bat.

7. Sandra got out her **pen** and began to write.

   A.   The goats were put in a pen.

   B.   Do you have a pen I can borrow?

   C.   The dog ran around in his pen.

   D.   The pen was big enough to hold ten horses.

8. Susan stretched the rubber band so far I thought it would **snap**.

   A.   Billy took a bite of the ginger snap cookie.

   B.   I had a hard time closing the snap on my shirt.

   C.   The teacher will snap at me if I don't hand in my paper.

   D.   We knew the rope would snap if we tried to swing from it.

9. The bird spread his wings to **fly** up into the sky.

   A.   A rocket can fly through the sky at incredible speeds.

   B.   My grandpa likes to go fly-fishing on the river.

   C.   The fly buzzed around the soda can.

   D.   Brenden teased, "Your fly is open."

10. The man had an angry look on his **face**.

   A.   The teacher told us to face to chalk board.

   B.   The sharp wind made her face cold and red.

   C.   He climbed the sheer face of the mountain.

   D.   You should always face your problems head on.

Chapter 8
Words—Roots, Prefixes, & Suffixes

This chapter covers Georgia standard

ELA3R2-e	Identifies and infers meaning from common root words, common prefixes (e.g., un-, re-, dis-, in-), and common suffixes (e.g., -tion, -ous, -ly).

ROOTS, PREFIXES, AND SUFFIXES—BREAKING DOWN WORDS

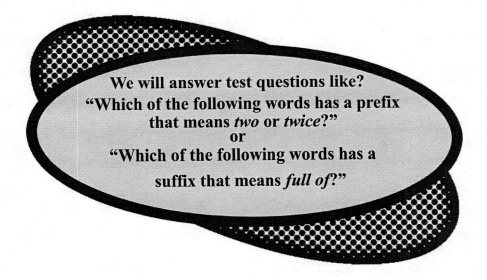

We will answer test questions like?
"Which of the following words has a prefix that means *two* or *twice*?"
or
"Which of the following words has a suffix that means *full of*?"

Learning about **roots**, **prefixes**, and **suffixes** is another way to understand new words. A word can be broken down into parts.

These parts are called the:

- prefix   • root   • suffix

Words—Roots, Prefixes, & Suffixes

 Not every word has a prefix, and not every word has a suffix. But every word is at least a root! A root can have both a prefix and suffix added to it.

- The **first part of a word** is the **prefix**.

- The **main part of a word** is the **root**.

- The **last part of a word** is the **suffix**.

For example, look at the word *dishonestly*:

Prefix:	Root:	Suffix:
dis	honest	ly
Dis is the prefix	**honest** is the root	and **ly** is the suffix

Learning the meanings of **roots, prefixes,** and **suffixes** will help you understand new words.

<u>Root:</u>

The **main** part of a word is the **root**. New words can be made out of root words by adding beginnings (prefixes) and endings (suffixes).

<u>**For example**</u>: *clear* is a root word. By adding prefixes and suffixes you can make new words

Example: un**clear**, **clear**ly, **clear**ed
These new words come from a **root word**.

Chapter 8

Here are a few root words and their meanings:

Root Word:	Meaning:	Example:
annu, anni	year	*annu*al, *anni*versary
aqua	water	*aqua*rium
audio	to hear	*audi*ble
bio	life	*bio*logy
deca	ten	*deca*de
multi	many	*multi*ply
path	feeling	*path*etic, sym*path*ize
phon	sound	tele*phon*e

Prefix:

The **prefix** is at the beginning of a word.

Prefixes are **always** attached to a root word.

Here are a few common prefixes and their meanings:

Prefix:	Meaning:	Example:
bi–	two or twice	*bi*-annual (every two years), *bi*lingual (someone who speaks two languages), *bi*cycle (a bike with two wheels)
dis–	to take away, the opposite of	*dis*respect (to take away respect)

Words—Roots, Prefixes, & Suffixes

mis–	wrong or badly	*mis*behave, *mis*inform, *mis*take
re–	to do again	*re*view, *re*read, *re*play
tri–	three	*tri*cycle (bike with three wheels) *tri*plets (three babies)
un-, in-, im-	not	*un*able, *in*formal (not formal), *im*possible

Practice 1:   Roots and Prefixes

ELA3R2-e

Read the following questions and choose the best answers. The first one is done for you.

1. What does the prefix *re-* in *recharge* mean?
   A.   full of
   B.   not
   C.   to do again
   D.   before

C is the correct answer. The prefix *re-* means to do again. So, recharge means "charge again."

2. A prefix is
   A.   always at the end of a root word.
   B.   never attached to a root word.
   C.   always at the beginning of a root word.
   D.   the root word.

3. How many colors would there be in a *tri*color shirt?
   A.   five   B.   four   C.   three   D.   two

4. What prefix would you add to the word "historic" to make it mean "before recorded history"?
    A. dis-   B. pre-   C. mis-   D. un-

5. What prefix would you add to the word "clean" to make it mean "not clean"?

    A. bi-   B. tri-   C. un-   D. re-

Suffix:

The suffix is at the end of a word.

Suffixes **are always** attached to a root word.

Here are a few common suffixes and their meanings:

Suffix:	Meaning:	Example:
–er	someone who does something or whose job it is	runn*er*, bak*er*, garden*er*
–ful	full of	cheer*ful*, plenti*ful*, fright*ful*, help*ful*, care*ful*
–less	without	fear*less* (someone without fear)
–ly	like, in the manner of	quiet*ly*, easi*ly*, hopeless*ly*
–ment	an act or instance of doing something or state of being	entertain*ment*, amaze*ment*, content*ment*
–ous	full of or having	spaci*ous* (a house with a lot of room), graci*ous* (someone full of kindness)

Practice 2:   Roots and Suffixes

ELA3R2-e

1. A suffix is

   A.   always at the beginning of a root word.

   B.   always at the end of a root word.

   C.   a root word.

   D.   never attached to a root word.

2. Which of the following suffixes means "someone who does something"?
   A.   -er   B.   -less   C.   -ous   D.   -ly

3. Which suffix would you add to the word *home* to make it mean "someone without a home"?
   A.   -er   B.   -less   C.   -ly   D.   -ful

4. If you add the suffix *-ous* to the root word *joy*, the new word, *joyous*, means
   A.   a maker of joy   C.   full of joy
   B.   an act of joy   D.   without joy

CHAPTER 8 SUMMARY

Root—The main part of a word is the root.

- **Prefix**—The prefix is at the beginning of a word. Prefixes are always attached to a root word.

- **Suffix**—The suffix is at the end of a word. Suffixes are always attached to a root word.

Chapter 8

LET'S REVIEW

ELA3R2-e

Read the sentences below and answer the questions.

1. Which of the following words has a **prefix** that means "in the wrong way"?

    A. misspell   B. retry   C. invisible   D. disgust

2. Which of the following words has a **suffix** that means "without"?
    A. farmer   B. careless   C. excitedly   D. cheerful

3. Which of the following words has a **prefix** that means "to do again"?
    A. luckless   B. happily   C. reheat   D. prevail

4. Which of the following words has a **prefix** that means "wrongly or badly"?
    A. mislead   B. gracious   C. unable   D. dislike

5. What **suffix** would you add to the word *fear* to make it mean "full of fear"?
    A. -ly   B. -er   C. -less   D. -ful

6. What does the **root** *phon* in *megaphone* mean?
    A. silent   B. ten   C. three   D. sound

7. What does the **root** word *multi* mean?
    A. full of   C. someone who does something
    B. many   D. two or twice

8. Which of the following words has a **prefix** that means to "take away"?
    A. disable   B. repeat   C. misguided   D. undo

Words—Roots, Prefixes, & Suffixes

9. What **suffix** would you add to the word *sleep* to make it mean "without sleep"?
   A. -er B. -ly C. -less D. -ful

10. What does the **root** word *deca* mean?
   A. three C. five
   B. two D. ten

Chapter 9
Words—Homonyms, Synonyms, & Antonyms

This chapter covers Georgia standards

ELA3R2-c	Recognizes and applies the appropriate usage of homophones, homographs, antonyms, and synonyms.
ELA3R2-f	Determines the meaning of unknown words on the basis of context.

Homonyms are words that look or sound alike but mean different things. There are different kinds of homonyms.:

Homophones:	Words that sound alike
Homographs:	Words that are spelled alike but have different meanings

HOMOPHONES—WORDS THAT SOUND THE SAME

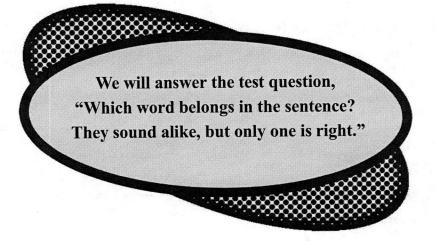

We will answer the test question, "Which word belongs in the sentence? They sound alike, but only one is right."

Words—Homonyms, Synonyms, & Antonyms

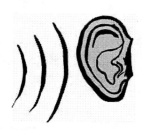

Homophones are words that sound the same but have different spellings and meanings. For example, the words *two*, *to*, and *too* sound the same. But they are spelled differently and have different meanings.

"I have **two** brothers."

"She is walking **to** school today."

"Your radio is **too** loud."

Listed below are a few more examples of homophones:

dear (as in "Dear Grandma")

deer (an animal that lives in the woods)

there (in that place)

their (belonging to them)

they're (short way to say *they are*)

your (belonging to you)

you're (short way to say *you are*)

know (to have information about something, to recognize someone)

no (the opposite of *yes*)

Chapter 9

Practice 1: Homophones

ELA3R2-c, f

Read the sentences below. Choose the correct word to complete each sentence.

1. I _____ so much food for dinner I could barely walk.
   A. ate   B. eight

2. A spider has _____ legs.
   A. ate   B. eight

3. What did you say? I didn't _____ what you said.
   A. here   B. hear

4. I found the keys right over _____.
   A. here   B. hear

5. We couldn't _____ the music because everyone was yelling.
   A. here   B. hear

6. The contest will take place _____ at the school.
   A. here   B. hear

7. In this picture, the water in the _____ is blue.
   A. see   B. sea

8. Tim can't _____ very well without his glasses.
   A. see   B. sea

9. The wind _____ in trees and made the leaves fall down.
   A. blue   B. blew

10. Teko's room is painted _____.
    A. blue   B. blew

HOMOGRAPHS—WORDS THAT LOOK THE SAME

ELA3R2-c, f

Like homophones, **homographs** sometimes sound the same, but sometimes they don't. Either way, homographs look the same but have different meanings.

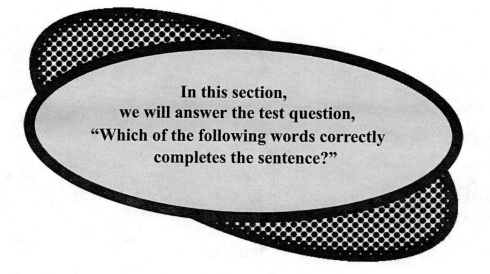

In this section,
we will answer the test question,
"Which of the following words correctly
completes the sentence?"

For example, look at these words:

- **does** (to do)

  "Why **does** Jake always wear a baseball cap?"

- **does** (female deer)

  "We saw three **does** and a buck in the woods."

Chapter 9

These words are spelled the same way. They look exactly alike. But, when they are used in a sentence, you can tell they have different meanings.

Here are a few more examples of homographs:

• **well:**   The **well** has been dry for years.   Jimmy doesn't feel **well** today.
• **left:**   Make a **left** turn.   My Grandma **left** yesterday.
• **can:**   You **can** do it!   Open the **can** of fruit.

Practice 2:   Homographs

ELA3R2-c, f

Look at the list of words below. Choose the right word to correctly complete each sentence.

Hint: each word is used twice.

    shower   tear   nail   sink   bat

1. After we ate dinner, I put the dishes in the _____.

    A. shower   B. nail   C. sink   D. bat

2. Cody held the _____ firmly, waiting for the pitch.

    A. shower   B. tear   C. nail   D. bat

Words—Homonyms, Synonyms, & Antonyms

3. The _____ flew out of the dark cave, scaring all of us.

     A. shower   B. tear   C. sink   D. bat

4. I take a _____ every night to wash up before going to bed.

     A. shower   B. nail   C. sink   D. bat

5. The little boat had a leak and began to _____ into the lake.

     A. shower   B. tear   C. nail   D. sink

6. She painted the _____ of her big toe bright pink.

     A. tear   B. nail   C. sink   D. bat

7. Matt had to pound a ____ into the wall to hang the picture.

     A. shower   B. tear   C. nail   D. bat

8. I didn't shed one _____ when we watched the sad movie.

     A. shower   B. tear   C. sink   D. bat

9. The rain _____ lasted for only a few minutes.

     A. shower   B. tear   C. nail   D. bat

10. The dress had a small _____ in it.

     A. shower   B. tear   C. sink   D. bat

Now, choose the **correct** definition for the underlined word in each sentence.

A. wind: a breeze
B. wind: turn a little wheel to make something work

11. The **wind** blew in my hair. A or B?

12. My grandpa has a watch that he has to **wind** every day. A or B?

A. park: to pull a car in to a space
B. park: a place to play

13. Aunt Katie took me and my friend Kyle to the **park** yesterday. A or B?

14. She had to **park** three blocks away because there was no room near the entrance. A or B?

SYNONYMS—WORDS THAT MEAN THE SAME THING

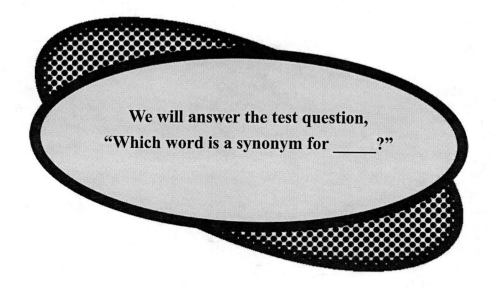

We will answer the test question,
"Which word is a synonym for _____?"

Synonyms are words that have the same or almost the same meaning. They are twins!

Examples:

- *Large* is a synonym for *big*.
- *Little* is a synonym for *small*.
- *Giggle* is a synonym for *laugh*.
- *Jump* is a synonym for *leap*.

Chapter 9

ANTONYMS—WORDS THAT HAVE THE OPPOSITE MEANING

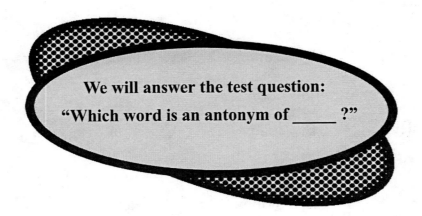

We will answer the test question:
"Which word is an antonym of _____ ?"

Antonyms are words that have the opposite meaning.

Examples:

- *Hot* is an antonym for *cold*.
- *Tall* is an antonym for *short*.
- *Day* is an antonym for *night*.
- *Big* is an antonym for *little*.

When you have to identify a synonym or antonym on the CRCT, just remember that **synonym means the same** (*synonym* and *same* both start with an **s**) and **antonym means opposite**. Let's practice.

Practice 3: Synonyms and Antonyms

ELA3R2-c, f

Read the sentences and answer the questions. The first one has been done for you.

1. Which word is an **antonym** of *happy*?

    A. cheerful   B. joyful   C. sad   D. pleased

If you said C, you're right! *Sad* is the opposite of *happy*. They are antonyms. Good job!

Words—Homonyms, Synonyms, & Antonyms

2. Which word is a **synonym** for *sick*?

    A. healthy   B. strong   C. fit   D. ill

3. Which word is a **synonym** for *easy*?

    A. simple   B. hard   C. difficult   D. tough

4. Which word is an **antonym** of *quiet*?

    A. silent   B. loud   C. hush   D. peaceful

5. Which word is an **antonym** of *dirty*?

    A. messy   B. sloppy   C. clean   D. filthy

6. Which word is a **synonym** for *strong*?

    A. powerful   B. weak   C. unhealthy   D. unfit

7. Which word is a **synonym** for *afraid*?

    A. brave   B. fearless   C. daring   D. scared

8. Which word is an **antonym** of *new*?

    A. fresh   B. latest   C. recent   D. old

9. Which word is an **antonym** for *nice*?

    A. friendly   B. kind   C. mean   D. cheerful

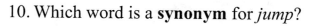

10. Which word is a **synonym** for *jump*?

    A. leap   B. still   C. frozen   D. unmoving

Chapter 9

On the next pages are two activities using antonyms and synonyms. In the crossword puzzle, choose an antonym of the numbered word to fill in the squares (for example, for 1 Across, choose an antonym of *happy*). In the word find puzzle, choose a synonym, and then circle it.

Antonym Crossword Puzzle

Across:

1. Happy
2. Strong
3. Healthy
4. Old
5. Mean

Down:

1. Afraid
2. Hard
3. Loud
4. Dirty
5. Moving

Synonym Word Find

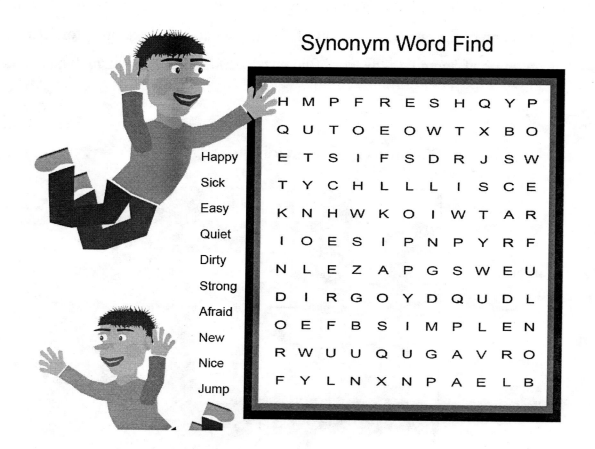

Happy
Sick
Easy
Quiet
Dirty
Strong
Afraid
New
Nice
Jump

```
H M P F R E S H Q Y P
Q U T O E O W T X B O
E T S I F S D R J S W
T Y C H L L I S C E
K N H W K O I W T A R
I O E S I P N P Y R F
N L E Z A P G S W E U
D I R G O Y D Q U D L
O E F B S I M P L E N
R W U U Q U G A V R O
F Y L N X N P A E L B
```

CHAPTER 9 SUMMARY

Homophones—words that **sound the same** but have different spellings and meanings.

Homographs—words that are spelled the same but have different meanings.

Synonyms—words that have the same or almost the same meaning.

Antonyms—words that have opposite meaning.

Don't Forget!

Chapter 9

LET'S REVIEW

ELA3R2-c, f

Read the sentences below and answer the questions.

1. Sally climbed the _____ quickly. She wanted to make it up to her room before her little sister did.

   A. stares   B. stairs

2. Megan gave me directions to her house. We have to make a _____ turn into her neighborhood.

   A. right   B. write

3. Paper is made out of _____.

   A. would   B. wood

4. What word means the **same** thing as *solution*?

   A. easy   B. problem   C. answer   D. puzzle

5. Which word means the **opposite** of *hungry*?

   A. starving   B. full   C. family   D. empty

6. Look at the two sentences below:

"Cindy took a bow at the end of the performance."

"Michael put a bow on top of the birthday present."

Words—Homonyms, Synonyms, & Antonyms

The word "**bow**" in these sentences is an example of

    A. a synonym.   C. a homophone.

    B. an antonym.   D. a homograph.

7. Which word is a **synonym** for *unhurt*?

    A. wounded   B. safe   C. injured   D. sick

Each sentence below has two **homographs**. One of the homographs is underlined. Choose the definition that matches the underlined word.

8. I shed a <u>tear</u> over the tear in my dress.
    A. crying or weeping   B. a rip

9. Jim wound the bandage around the bleeding <u>wound</u> on his hand.
    A. to wrap or cover   B. a cut or an injury

10. After the cat fell into the <u>well</u>, she didn't feel well for a few days.
    A. a hole in the ground   B. being in good health

Chapter 10
Understanding Genres—Fiction and Nonfiction

This chapter covers Georgia standard

ELA3R3-n	Identifies the basic elements of a variety of genres (fiction, nonfiction, drama, and poetry.)

On the CRCT Reading test, you will be asked to identify types of literature. You will see questions like, "What kind of story is this?" and "Is this passage fiction or nonfiction?"

In this chapter, you will learn how to answer these questions. You will learn about fiction and nonfiction. Then, in the next two chapters, you will also learn about drama and poetry.

WHAT IS A GENRE?

Imagine that you are going to the mall. You need to buy a new pair of shoes. A shoe store is one kind of store in the mall. The shoe store has all kinds of shoes. There are boots, sandals, tennis shoes, and so on. They are all shoes, but they are different types of shoes. The types are grouped together by what they have in common. For example, boots are all called boots because they cover your ankle or part of your leg, which shoes don't.

Literature is put into groups just like shoes are. Types of literature are called **genres**. Genre is a fancy word for *type* or *kind*.

There are four main genres (types) of literature. They are **fiction**, **nonfiction**, **drama**, and **poetry**. These are big genres (like stores in a mall). They have little genres in them (like the types of things each store sells).

Understanding Genres—Fiction and Nonfiction

Here's how it works.

Big Genre	**Store in the Mall**
Fiction	Shoe Store
Little Genres (types) of Fiction	**Types of Shoes in the Shoe Store**
Fable	Ballet Slippers
Fairytale	Boots
Fantasy	Clogs
Legend	High Heels
Mystery	Mules
Myth	Running Shoes
Science Fiction	Sandals
Tall Tale	Tennis Shoes

Big Genre	**Store in the Mall**
Nonfiction	Sports Store

Little Genres (types) of Nonfiction	**Types of Things in the Sports Store**
Advertisement	Basketballs
Article	Baseballs
Autobiography	Catcher's Mitts
Biography	Hockey Sticks
History	Soccer Balls
How-to Article or Book	Skateboards
Letter	Skates
Speech	Tennis Rackets

MORE ABOUT FICTION

What is **fiction**? It is the name for made-up stories. Fiction stories have characters, places, and events that are all made up by the author. Some fiction stories have real people or places in them. But what happens in the story is invented by the author.

There are many genres (types) of fiction. Some fiction is long. It can be a whole book. For example, it can be a novel like *Fly Away Home* by Eve Bunting. It might take you many days to read it. Some fiction is short. For example, it can be a short fable like "The Tortoise and the Hare" by Aesop. It might take you only a few minutes to read it.

GENRES OF FICTION

Here are some of the kinds of fiction:

Genre	Description	Examples
Fable	a short story with a lesson in it; fables often have talking animals as characters	Aesop's fables
Fairytale	usually starts with "once upon a time' and ends with "happily ever after," usually has magic in it	"Cinderalla," "Goldilocks and the Three Bears"
Legend	a story about the history of a place or people; like a tall tale, it can have real people in it; a legend tells something important about the place or people it is about	the legend of the Fountain of Youth, the legend of Pocahontas

Genre	Description	Examples
Mystery	a story with characters who have to solve a puzzle or crime	*Scoop Snoops* by Constance Hiser *Mystery Ranch* by Gertrude Warner
Myth	a myth is a story with supernatural characters (people and animals with special powers) that explains something in nature	stories about how the earth was created or how certain animals came to be; Green mythology, like the story of Pandora and her magic box
Science Fiction	a story with scientific facts or made-up science of the future; sometimes it has aliens or takes place on another planet	*Ned Feldman, Space Pirate* by Daniel Pinkwater *The Time Machine* by H. G. Wells
Tall Tale	a short story with larger-than-life heroes; sometimes tall tales are based on real people, but the stories are made up and sometimes are very funny	"Paul Bunyan Tames the Whistling River," "The Saga of Pecos Bill"

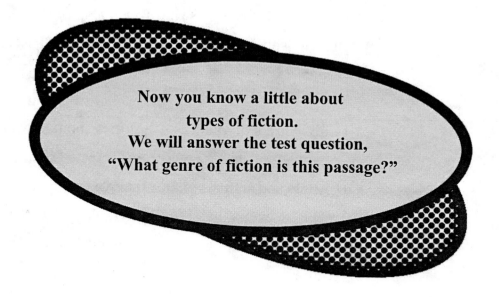

Now you know a little about
types of fiction.
We will answer the test question,
"What genre of fiction is this passage?"

Practice 1:   Genres of Fiction

ELA3R3-n

Read the passages below. All of the passages are fiction. But what kind of fiction are they? Choose the answer that BEST tells what genre (type) of fiction each one is. The first one has been done for you.

The Tiny Diver

One day, I went over to the fish bowl in my room. I was about to feed Jupiter, my pet goldfish. Jupe was swimming near the top of the bowl. This might sound silly—after all, he is a fish—but he looked scared. Then I saw something else in the bowl move.

A tiny little diver was at the bottom of the bowl. He stood next to the little fake castle on the bottom. Now, my sister could have just dropped a little toy diver in there…but he was MOVING! The diver was waving up at Jupe. He looked like he was trying to talk to my fish. Then he saw me.

128

I reached in and pulled him out. I was very careful not to crush the tiny guy. He stood on my desk and shook off the water. He then took off his little helmet.

"Greetings, earthling!" he said.

I must have fainted. I woke up hours later. I know it was much later because it was getting dark. I looked around. The little diver was sitting at the edge of the desk. I was so glad he had not disappeared.

"Who are you?" I asked him.

"I am Vorgon. I am from the planet Goloxo."

1. What **genre** (type) of fiction story is this?

   A.   myth

   B.   fantasy

   C.   legend

   D.   science fiction

Let's look at each answer. Could it be A? In the table about genres, you read that a myth is a story that explains something in nature. Does that fit this passage? Not really. What about answer B? That does not seem right. A fantasy story happens in a dream-like place, but the narrator's bedroom is pretty normal. Could it be C, a legend? Not really. It does not explain about a place or people from history. **Answer D is the best choice.** This passage is from a science fiction story. How do we know? The big clue is that there is a tiny alien in it!

My Self-Cleaning Room

Mom was mad at me. She said I better clean my room or there would be no swimming this weekend. With a big sigh, I shuffled to my room.

I opened the door and walked in. In my head, I was already planning to attack the piles of games, toys, clothes, and books. So it took me a minute to see what I saw. I could not believe what I saw. It was the floor. I could see the floor because everything was picked up.

Blinking, I backed up. Let's try again, I thought. I closed the door and opened it again. Yup, the room was CLEAN! But how did it happen?

I sat down on the floor. As I sat thinking, I pulled out some toys. I looked at a few books and left them on the floor. Then I decided: it must have been Mom.

I went to the kitchen where Mom was making dinner. "Sorry," I said, "that I didn't clean my room. But how come you did it?" She slowly turned to me.

"Me? Why would I clean your room?" she said. "That's your job." Then she laughed. "Oh, I see. You're being funny. Ok, let's see how well you did at cleaning."

Mom followed me to my room. I cringed because I thought maybe I had only imagined it was clean. She would walk in, and it would be messy again!

But there it was, spotless. Even the toys and books I had just pulled out were put away again! What was going on here? All these things weren't putting themselves away!

Or were they…?

2. What **genre** of fiction is this passage?
   A. fable   B. mystery   C. tall tale   D. legend

3. How can you tell that it's this genre?
   A. because there are talking animals in it
   B. because it has a larger-than-life hero
   C. because there is a puzzling event to solve
   D. because it has supernatural characters

NONFICTION—STORIES ABOUT REAL PEOPLE AND EVENTS

Nonfiction means "not fiction." Nonfiction is about real people, places, and events. Nothing is made up. It is real and true. It tells about real life. Sometimes it is about the past. Other times, it is about things happening now or people living now. There are many genres of nonfiction. Here are some of them.

Genre	Description	Examples
Advertisement	a notice about a service or product	job notices in the newspaper, a full-page ad in a magazine that tells you about new Transformers toys available in stores
Article	short writing in a newspaper of magazine about a real event or topic	"Dog Rescues Owner from Fire' in the local newspaper, "What to See When You Visit Rome" in a travel magazine
Autobiography	the story of a real person's life written by that person; the word "I" is used because the person is writing about his or her own life	*Anne Frank: The Diary of a Young Girl* by Anne Frank, *Africa in My Blood: An Autobiography in Letters* by Jane Goodall
Biography	the story of a real person's life written by someone else; the word "he" or "she" is used because the author is writing about another person	*The Story of Benjamin Franklin* by Margaret Davidson *Joan of Arc* by Diane Stanley

Understanding Genres—Fiction and Nonfiction

Genre	Description	Examples
History	an article or a book about one or more events in the past	*The Reb and the Redcoats* by Constance Savery *The Scottish Chiefs* by Jane Porter
How-to Article or Book	writing that tells you how to do a thing or make a thing	"Making a Kite" article in a magazine, *180 Days of Manners* (about how to have good manners) by Donna Forrest and Jenny Meng*er*
Letter	personal writing from one person to another; there are also letters to the editor in newspapers and magazines, which are letters that readers write and want to get published for other people to read	a letter you write to your grandmother, a letter published in the newspaper that tells the author's opinion about a new shop in town, or even an email or My Space message to a friend
Speech	writing down what you want to say out loud; if you will speak in class, you might jot down on a note card what you will talk about	the president's State of the Union Address that's shown on TV; "The Gettysburg Address" by Abraham Lincoln

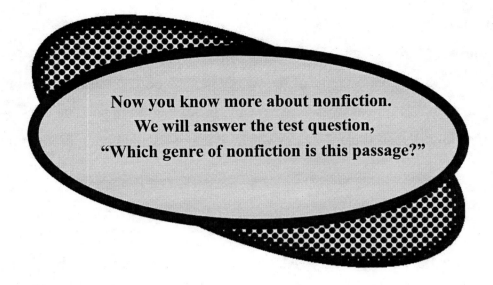

Now you know more about nonfiction.
We will answer the test question,
"Which genre of nonfiction is this passage?"

Practice 2: Genres of Nonfiction

ELA3R3-n

Read these passages. All of them are nonfiction. For each passage, decide what kind of nonfiction it is. Choose the genre that fits BEST. The first one has been done for you.

George Washington

George Washington grew up on a farm in Virginia. As a little boy, he really liked math. He worked hard on the farm. He got big and strong. His parents taught him to be honest and always tell the truth.

George Washington

When he grew up, George helped explore the country. He made maps of places that had no maps yet. He was a soldier, too. He fought to protect the settlers in the colonies. He became a great general when America fought to be free from British rule.

George Washington became the first President of the United States. The nation's capitol—Washington, D.C.—is named for him. He was a very good President. Today, he is known as "The Father of our Country."

Understanding Genres—Fiction and Nonfiction

1. This passage is
   A. a biography.
   B. an autobiography.
   C. a how-to article.
   D. an advertisement.

Did you choose A? You're right! This is a biography. Someone else is writing about George Washington. You know this because of the word "he." George Washington is not writing about himself, so it can't be answer B. Answer C is not right: the passage does not tell you how to do something. And it can't be answer D: it is not an ad about a product or service.

Who Am I?

I was born in Tuskegee, Alabama, in 1913. At that time, blacks and whites were separated. Blacks were not allowed to do some things. For example, on the bus, blacks could not sit down when whites were standing.

One day, I was on a bus. I was tired and had to sit down. I did not give up my seat to a white person. The police arrested me for disobeying the law. Many blacks did not like that I got arrested. So they had a bus boycott. That means the blacks did not ride the bus. Dr. Martin Luther King, Jr., even helped with the boycott.

Many people call me brave. I am glad that my actions helped end segregation (separation of blacks and whites). I later worked in the United States House of Representatives. I always tried to do good things to help African Americans. My name is Rosa Parks.

Now, try some more on your own.

2. This passage is
   A. an advertisement.
   B. a biography.
   C. an autobiography.
   D. a how-to article.

Try new *Bright White* toothpaste! It is the best toothpaste! It tastes good. It makes your teeth white. It makes

your breath smell fresh. You will love brushing your teeth. So get some *Bright White* today!

3. This passage is an example of
   A. a letter.
   B. a history.
   C. a biography.
   D. an advertisement.

> To the Editor:
>
> You should have more photos in your magazine. The articles are fun. But you need to show what they talk about. I read one article about ant hills. There was no picture of an ant hill with it. It told how big ant hills get, but it would be great to see how big they are. Pictures would be very helpful.
>
> Thanks you for listening.
>
> Yours truly,
>
> Josh Jones

4. This passage is an example of
   A. a letter.   B. an article.   C. a speech.   D. a history.

Now, let's talk more about the difference between the big genres of fiction and nonfiction.

THE DIFFERENCE BETWEEN FICTION AND NONFICTION

In chapter 6, you learned about **fact** and **opinion**. A fact is true. It can be proven. An opinion is a feeling or belief. It can't be proven.

Understanding Genres—Fiction and Nonfiction

The difference between fiction and nonfiction is almost the same. When you read a passage, ask yourself: "Is this true? Is it about a real event that happened? Is it about a real person?" If yes, then the passage is most likely nonfiction.

If the passage is imaginary or made up, it is most likely fiction. Now that you know a little more about nonfiction and fiction, let's practice.

We will answer the test question,
"Is this passage fiction or nonfiction?"

Practice 3: Fiction and Nonfiction

ELA3R3-n

See if you can tell the difference between fiction and nonfiction. Don't worry! The first one is done for you.

1. Which of the following is nonfiction?

    A. a book on the history of England
    B. a fairytale about an ogre
    C. a myth about the moon
    D. a mystery novel

If you picked A, you're right on target! Good job! In the lesson about nonfiction, we learned that histories are nonfiction. The other answers are all fiction. They are made-up or make-believe stories. They are not based on real people, events, places, or animals. Try some more questions.

2. Which of the following is fiction?
    A. a book about the birds of Africa
    B. an article about thunderstorms
    C. a story about a talking, flying pig
    D. a book on how to take care of kittens

3. Look at the book titles below. Decide which one is fiction.
    A. *Heroes of the Civil War*
    B. *How to Speak Spanish*
    C. *The Blue Fairy Book*
    D. *Our Solar System*

4. Which of the following is nonfiction?
    A. a scary ghost story
    B. the legend of Big Foot
    C. a play about a fiery dragon
    D. a book about planting a garden

CHAPTER 10 SUMMARY

Genre—a fancy word that means a type or a kind of literature. There are four main genres (types) of literature: fiction, nonfiction, drama, and poetry.

Nonfiction—stories about real people or real events. Nothing is made up in nonfiction books.

Examples of **nonfiction** are:

Advertisement	Autobiography
History	Letter
Article	Biography
How-to Article or Book	Speech

Fiction—stories about imaginary people, animals, and places. A fiction story is made up or created by the author. Examples of **fiction** are:

Fable	Fantasy
Mystery	Science Fiction
Fairytale	Legend
Myth	Tall Tale

LET'S REVIEW

ELA3R3-n

Read the passages and answer the questions.

The Ant and the Dove

An Ant went to the bank of a river to quench its thirst. He was carried away by the rush of the stream. He was close to drowning! A Dove sitting in a tree near the water plucked a leaf and let it fall into the stream. The Ant climbed onto it and floated safely to the bank. Shortly afterwards a bird catcher came and stood under the tree. He set a trap for the Dove, which sat in the branches. The Ant saw the bird catcher and what he was doing. Quickly, the Ant crawled over and stung him in the foot. In pain, the bird catcher threw down the trap, and the noise made the Dove fly away.

The lesson of the story? One good turn deserves another.

Chapter 10

1. What genre of fiction is this?

   A. science fiction

   B. mystery

   C. legend

   D. fable

2. What is one way that you can tell it's this genre of fiction?

   A. because there is magic in it

   B. because it explains something strange

   C. because it has a lesson

   D. because it happens on another planet

Terrible Lizards!

The name dinosaur means "terrible lizard." Dinosaurs lived about 200 million years ago. They were the biggest lizards to ever walk the earth. Even though dinosaurs were huge, most of them were harmless. Many of them ate only plants. But, there were a few terrible ones. The Tyrannosaurus Rex was one the fiercest dinosaurs of them all. The T-Rex was 19 to 20 feet tall. That's as big as a house! It had sharp teeth and big claws to help it catch and eat its prey.

3. The passage above is an example of which genre of nonfiction?

   A. history

   B. biography

   C. letter

   D. advertisement

4. How do you know what genre this is?

   A. because it tells about a real person from the past

   B. because it talks about products you can buy

   C. because it had opinions about a topic

   D. because it is about events in the past

Harry Houdini

Harry Houdini was a magician. He did magic tricks and risky stunts. He would tie himself up and hang upside down from a crane. Minutes later, he would escape. Sometimes he would tie his hands and go into a glass box. The box would be locked and filled with water while he was in it. Seconds later, he would come out, alive and well.

5. This passage is
   A. a myth.
   B. a legend.
   C. a biography.
   D. a how-to article.

6. How can you tell it is this kind of passage?
   A. It tells why something in nature happens.
   B. It is about a real person from the past.
   C. It is made up by the author.
   D. It tells how to escape.

7. Which of the following is nonfiction?
   A. a story about a pot of gold at the end of a rainbow
   B. a fairytale about a princess and a unicorn
   C. a book about the founding fathers of America
   D. a play about a statue coming to life

8. These are some books in a library. Somehow, a fiction book got into the nonfiction section. Choose the fiction book that needs to be put back to its place in the fiction section.
   A. *Benjamin Franklin: The Father of Electricity*
   B. *The Animals of the Rain Forest*
   C. *How to Build a Fort*
   D. *The Frog Prince*

Chapter 11
Understanding Genres—Drama

This chapter covers Georgia standard

ELA3R3-n	Identifies the basic elements of a variety of genres (fiction, nonfiction, drama, and poetry).

In chapter 10, you saw that there are four big genres of literature: fiction, nonfiction, drama, and poetry. Then, you read about fiction and nonfiction. Now, you'll learn about drama.

DRAMA—NOW, THAT'S ACTING!

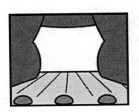

A **drama** is a play. Dramas are written to be acted out on a stage. Actors and actresses play the characters. But you can read it, too, just like a story. When you see it written, drama is easy to pick out. It looks very different from other writing.

A drama has a list of characters at the start. It is arranged into acts and scenes. These are a little like the chapters of a book. Here is an example of a three-act play:

Act 1
    Scene 1 Toby's house
    Scene 2 Toby's Backyard
Act 2
    Scene 1 The next day, at school
    Scene 2 On the playground
Act 3
    Scene 1 Same day, back at Toby's house
    Scene 2 Toby's bedroom
    Scene 3 The kitchen at Toby's house

Some short plays only have one or two acts. Some have only acts and no scenes to break them up further.

Understanding Genres—Drama

In a book or a story, the author tells you about the setting. The narrator describes where the story is happening. In a play, there is no narrator. So, the author tells you where each scene is going on in **stage directions**.

What happens in the play is written in parentheses ( ) or brackets [ ]. The words in these brackets are called stage directions. Stage directions tell you things like where the furniture is in a scene and where the characters are on stage. They also tell you how each character looks and talks and what he or she does.

But most of the play is made up of **dialogue**. Dialogue is when characters talk to each other. In a drama, the characters tell the story by talking. Look at the example below.

Characters

Jimmy, a nine-year-old boy

Carson, Jimmy's little brother

Buckey, Jimmy's friend

Mr. Stunky, a mean old man

Act 1, Scene 1

(A neighborhood. Jimmy, Carson, and Buckey are playing soccer in the street. Jimmy kicks the ball hard. The ball lands behind the fence in Mr. Stunky's backyard.)

BUCKEY: I can't believe you kicked it over there! We're never going to finish the game.

JIMMY: I'll get it. We can finish the game.

CARSON *(looking scared)*: No, Jimmy. Don't get it. You'd have to climb the fence.

BUCKEY: Yeah, Mr. Stunky might have a big mean dog back there. Or worse, maybe a man-eating monkey with big teeth *(Buckey makes a scary face at Jimmy)*.

JIMMY: There is nothing behind Mr. Stunky's fence. Now, I'm going to get our ball. *(Jimmy starts walking toward Mr. Stunky's fence.)*

Do you see how different a drama looks from a story or a book? Take note of the stage directions and what they show you. Did you see how the characters told the story as they talked?

Practice 1: Drama

> ELA3R3-n

Answer these questions about drama.

1. Drama is
   A. an actor.   B. an act.   C. a play.   D. a scene.

2. In a drama, how a character looks and feels is usually
   A. in parentheses or brackets.   C. very serious.
   B. in the list of characters.   D. left out.

3. Where can you find the list of characters?
   A. at the end of the play   C. at the beginning of the play
   B. in the middle of the play   D. there is no list of characters

4. A drama is arranged
   A. by the number of characters.   C. in dialogue and directions.
   B. in acts and scenes.   D. by what's going on.

5. A drama is meant to be
   A. read from back to front.   C. fun and amusing.
   B. performed on a stage.   D. sad and serious.

GENRES OF DRAMA—COMEDY AND TRAGEDY

 Just like fiction and nonfiction, drama is a big genre of literature. Like the other big genres, it has little genres or types. The main two types of drama are **comedy** and **tragedy**.

Some drama starts out as drama. An author writes a play to be acted on stage. Also, a play can be made up from a story you already know. For example, "Beauty and the Beast" was written as a fairytale. Then, a playwright (a person who writes plays) took the story and turned it into a play. Then it was turned into a movie, too! A movie is just a different kind of drama. The written play for a movie or TV show is called a screenplay.

A **comedy** is a play that makes you feel good. It can make you laugh. But even if isn't funny, it has a happy ending. At the end of a comedy, the main character gets what he or she wants or needs.

For example, a play of "A Christmas Carol" can be called a comedy. It has some scary moments, and Scrooge is mean at the start. But in the end, he turns into a nice person. As the main character, he gets what he really wants—he was a miser and wanted riches, but he gets the best riches in the world, the love of his family and friends.

A **tragedy** is a play that is usually serious. Sometimes it can have funny events or characters. But the main idea is something sad or unlucky. At the end of a tragedy, the main character doesn't get what he or she wants or needs. Tragedies usually make people think about things. Sometimes they teach lessons.

Example: A play about "Goldilocks and the Three Bears" can be called a tragedy. The story has funny events and is fun to watch or read. But it does not really have a happy ending. Goldilocks eats the bears' food and breaks their furniture, so the bears are sad at the end. Goldilocks has to run away when the bears come home. So, she is not happy at the end either. A lesson of this drama could be, "You should not use other people's things without permission."

Chapter 11

Practice 2: Comedy and Tragedy

ELA3R3-n

Answer these questions about the two main genres of drama, comedy and tragedy.

1. A drama in which funny things happen but that does not have a happy ending is a
    A. comedy   B. tragedy

2. What kind of drama is it when the main character gets what he or she wants or needs?
    A. comedy.   B. tragedy.

Read this passage. Then, answer the questions that follow.

The Case of the Missing Diamond

Characters

Sherlock Holmes, the famous detective

Dr. Watson, his friend and assistant

Mrs. Twomy, who has had her diamond stolen

Rex, Mrs. Twomy's Golden Retriever

Act 3, Scene 3

SHERLOCK: Yes, it's true. I have discovered that there was a witness to the crime.

MRS. TWOMY [shocked]: Really? But who? Why hasn't this person come forward to tell us what happened to my diamond?

SHERLOCK: He tried, dear lady. Unfortunately, we do not understand his speech.

MRS. TWOMY: Oh, it's a foreigner. [She sounds annoyed when she says the word *foreigner.*]

SHERLOCK: Not at all, Madam. It is Rex. [He looks at Rex, who looks up at him.]

[Mrs. Twomy's eyes and mouth both get very round.]

DR. WATSON: But, Holmes, how can we find out what happened? As you said, the dog can't speak to us.

SHERLOCK: But the dog's nose is superior! Watch as he follows it to the thief's lair. [He takes the leash from Mrs. Twomy and points Rex to stage right. Rex sniffs at the ground and runs in that direction, with everyone following him.]

[Sounds of the hunt are heard from off stage.] SHERLOCK: There it is! Your diamond. Let us leave this place before the criminal returns. Scotland Yard will come back to arrest him. [They all return to the stage.]

MRS. TWOMY: Oh, Mr. Holmes. How can I ever thank you?

SHERLOCK: I rather think it is someone else that deserves the praise. [He looks down at Rex, who wags his tail. Sherlock, Mrs. Twomy, and Rex begin walking off stage.]

DR. WATSON [to no one in particular]: I hope that mutt gets a big, juicy bone tonight!

THE END

3. What genre of drama is this passage?
   A. comedy   B. tragedy

4. How can you tell that it's this genre?
   A. It has a sad ending.   C. It has a happy ending.
   B. There are only three characters.   D. There are funny events in it.

CHAPTER 11 SUMMARY

Drama—a play. A drama has a list of characters at the beginning. It is organized into scenes and acts.

Stage Directions—usually in parenthesis ( ) or brackets [ ], stage directions have descriptions of where the story is taking place and tell you character actions and expressions.

Dialogue—the main way the story is told in drama. Dialogue is the written words of what characters say to each other.

Comedy—a drama with a happy ending. The main character gets what he or she wants or needs.

Tragedy—a drama that is usually serious and does not have a happy ending. It might have funny events or characters in it. Sometimes it teaches a lesson.

LET'S REVIEW

ELA3R3-n

Katie, the Kid Genius

Characters

Katie, a third-grade student

Mrs. Stinch, the Principal

Mr. Fowler, a guidance counselor

Understanding Genres—Drama

(It is the early afternoon. Katie is sitting in a chair in the principal's office. She's nervously twisting her pony tail. She's waiting for Mrs. Stinch to walk into the room. She thinks she's in trouble. Mrs. Stinch walks in and sits at her desk.)

MRS. STINCH: Do you know why I called you to my office, Katie?

KATIE: *(nervously, swallowing hard)* No, ma'am. Am I in trouble?

MRS. STINCH: No. I called you here because we have the results of your test.

KATIE: *(looking relieved)* My test?

MRS. STINCH: Yes, the test you took last week. Mr. Fowler will be coming in to talk with you about it.

KATIE: *(looking worried again)* Mr. Fowler? The school counselor? Why does he need to talk to me?

(Mr. Fowler walks into the room. He has an armful of papers. He sits next to Katie)

MR. FOWLER: I'm sorry I'm late. *(looking at Mrs. Stinch)* Did you tell her?

(Mrs. Stinch shakes her head no)

KATIE: What? What is it?

MR. FOWLER: Well, Katie. That test you took…no one has ever passed it. But, you *(he smiles big)*, you didn't get one answer wrong. I called around to other schools. We all agree. Katie, you are a genius!

KATIE: *(looking stunned)* A genius? Like a mad scientist?

MR. FOWLER: No, you are an official genius. *(clapping his hands together)* The real deal.

KATIE: It can't be. *(still stunned)* I just want to be a kid.

Chapter 11

MRS. STINCH: Well, sorry kiddo. It looks like you're both. A kid and a genius.

KATIE: What does this mean? Will I have to go to…special classes? Leave my friends?

MRS. STINCH: Well, you'll take some advanced classes, yes. But you'll stay right here. What it means, however, is that you will be able to go to any college you want!

KATIE: Oh… *(she thought about all the things she wanted to do in life, and she smiled)*

THE END

1. This passage is an example of
   A. a three-act play.
   B. a one-act play.
   C. two acts.
   D. three scenes.

2. The author gives action and emotion to the characters by using
   A. big letters.
   B. parenthesis or brackets.
   C. periods.
   D. all capital letters.

3. What genre of drama is this?
   A. comedy   B. tragedy

4. How do we know it is this genre?
   A. because the main character is a bad person
   B. because it is about a real person's life
   C. because it has a list of characters
   D. because it has a happy ending

Understanding Genres—Drama

Read this part of the play. Then, answer the next two questions.

KATIE: *(looking relieved)* My test?

5. The words in parentheses are an example of
    A. dialogue.
    B. stage direction.
    C. a funny event.
    D. a scene.

6. The words "My test?" that Katie says are an example of
    A. dialogue.
    B. stage direction.
    C. a funny event.
    D. a scene.

7. In drama, dialogue is
    A. how the characters act and move.
    B. the reason plays are so short.
    C. the main way the story is told.
    D. a clue to show it is a comedy.

Chapter 12
Understanding Genres—Poetry

This chapter covers Georgia standard

ELA3R3-n	Identifies the basic elements of a variety of genres (fiction, nonfiction, drama, and poetry.)

POETRY—DOES IT HAVE TO RHYME?

Another genre of writing is poetry. **Poetry** expresses ideas and feelings in a creative way. Poetry does not have paragraphs. Sometimes it does not have commas, periods, or other punctuation. Some poetry rhymes. But it does not have to rhyme to be a poem.

Like drama, a poem looks very different from regular writing. A poem has lines instead of sentences. It has stanzas (groups of lines) instead of paragraphs. Poetry also can use capital letters in different ways than regular writing. We will look at all of this in this chapter.

RHYMING

Sometimes poetry **rhymes**. That means some words at the ends of the lines sound alike. For example, the words "hot" and "pot" rhyme. To see how rhyming words are used in a poem, see the words at the ends of lines.

LINES

Every poem has **lines**. Many times, there are numbers next to the poem that can help you count the lines in the poem.

Example:

"Who?"
by Emily Dickinson

1	My friend must be a bird,
2	Because it flies!
3	Mortal my friend must be,
4	Because it dies!
5	Barbs has it, like a bee.
6	Ah, curious friend,
7	Thou puzzlest me!

How many lines are in this poem? There are seven lines. If a question asks how many lines, just count them. Line numbers are also helpful when you are looking for other answers. For example, a question on a test might ask this:

"Which of these pairs of lines rhyme?"

   A. lines 1 and 2
   B. lines 3 and 4
   C. lines 2 and 4
   D. lines 6 and 7

The correct answer is "C" because line 2 ends with "flies" and line 4 ends with "dies." The other pairs of lines in the answer choices do not have rhyming words at their ends.

STANZAS

A **stanza** is a group of lines in a poem. Stanzas are usually set apart by a space.

Example:

There was a little turtle
Who lived in a box.
He swam in the puddles
And climbed on the rocks.   1st stanza

He snapped at the mosquito,
He snapped at the flea.
He snapped at the minnow,
And he snapped at me.   2nd stanza

He caught the mosquito,
He caught the flea.
He caught the minnow,
But he didn't catch me!   3rd stanza

There are three groups of lines in this poem. Each one is separated by a space. So, how many stanzas are in this poem? There are three. If a question asks how many stanzas there are in a poem, look for the space between a group of lines and count the stanzas.

CAPITAL LETTERS

Usually, each new line in a poem starts with a **capital letter**. Look at the two poems above. Notice how each line begins with a capital letter.

Some poets also use capital letters to give special attention to some words. For example, look at the following poem:

A Fly and a Flea in a Flue

by Anonymous

A Fly and a Flea in a Flue
Were imprisoned, so what could they do?
Said the fly, "Let us flee!"
"Let us fly!" said the flea,
And they flew through a flaw in the flue.

In the first line, the words *Fly*, *Flea*, and *Flue* all start with a capital letter. The poet did this to draw your attention to them. They also start with the same letter, *F*. Many other words in the poem also start with *F*. This gives an interesting sound effect to the poem.

Practice 1: Poetry

> **ELA3R3-n**

Read the poem below and answer the questions.

"The Lost Doll"

by Charles Kingsley

I once had a sweet little doll, dears,
    The prettiest doll in the world;
Her cheeks were so red and white, dears,
    And her hair was so charmingly curled.
But I lost my poor little doll, dears,
    As I played in the heath·one day;

5

154

And I cried for her more than a week, dears,
  But I never could find where she lay.

I found my poor little doll, dears,
  As I played in the heath one day;   10
Folks say she is terribly changed, dears,
  For her paint is all washed away,
And her arms trodden off by the cows, dears,
  And her hair not the least bit curled;
Yet for old sakes' sake, she is still, dears,   15
  The prettiest doll in the world.

Note: A heath is an area of open land with a lot of small shrubs and bushes on it.

1. How many stanzas are in this poem?
    A. 2   B. 3   C. 8   D. 16

2. How many lines are in this poem?
    A. 8   B. 16   C. 17   D. 20

3. What word is repeated at the END of every other line?
    A. "doll"   B. "heath"   C. "dears"   D. "I"

4. What is described as having red and white cheeks and "charmingly curled" hair?
    A. the heath   B. the speaker   C. a doll   D. a cow

5. What happened to the speaker's doll in the first stanza?
    A. It was stolen.   C. It was sold.
    B. It was lost.   D. It was found.

CHAPTER 12 SUMMARY

Poetry—A creative way to express ideas and feelings. A poem has stanzas, lines, and capital letters.

Lines—every poem has lines. Many times, there are numbers next to the poem that help you count the lines in each poem.

Stanzas—a stanza is a group of lines in a poem that is usually set apart by a space.

Capital Letters— in most poems, every new line starts with a capital letter.

LET'S REVIEW

ELA3R3-n

Ten Layer Cake

I built a ten layer cake
Out of twigs, berries and dates.
I put some water in mud
And used it as glue
To keep the layers up
On my layered thing-a-ma-do.

Chapter 12

I built it in the back yard
Right under my window
And sprinkled it with seeds,
To get the birds and squirrels to
Come take a nibble.

When I was finished
I watched from the window
As the animals came to taste my thing-a-ma-do.

The birds they flittered and pecked at the seeds
The squirrels they dug in and grabbed whatever they pleased
The chipmunks chipped away at the dates
but didn't care too much for the seeds the birds ate

But that night while I slept
The rain came down.
And when I looked out my window,
My ten layer cake was down.

Only the twigs remained
In a small pile on the wet ground.

Oh well, I thought,
As I got out of bed
I'll just have to build another cake
before the sun goes down.

Understanding Genres—Poetry

1. This passage is an example of
   A. a biography
   B. a drama
   C. a poem
   D. nonfiction

2. How many stanzas are in this poem?
   A. 1   B. 20   C. 5   D. 7

3. What happens to the ten layer cake at the end of the passage?
   A. it runs away from the birds
   B. it gets bigger
   C. it gets washed away by rain
   D. it comes to life

4. How many lines are in the 4th stanza?
   A. 4   B. 7   C. 9   D. 5

5. What kinds of animals came to eat the ten layer cake?
   A. squirrels
   B. chipmunks
   C. birds
   D. all of the above

Chapter 13
Characters, Plot, & Setting

This chapter covers Georgia standards

ELA3R3-e, f	Makes judgments and inferences about setting, characters, and events and supports them with evidence from the text.

WHAT MAKES A CHARACTER?

Every person is different. We all have qualities that make us who we are. The same is true for characters in a story. An author has to make characters different from one another so they seem "real" to readers. Making up all the details to make a character seem real is called **characterization**.

Authors tell us about characters in different ways. They can describe the people or animals in a story. **Description** tells how they look, how old they are, what they are wearing, and how they feel. Authors also have characters talk to each other. When characters talk to each other in a story, it is called **dialogue**. This shows how they treat other people. You can make judgments about characters based on how they are described and how they talk and act.

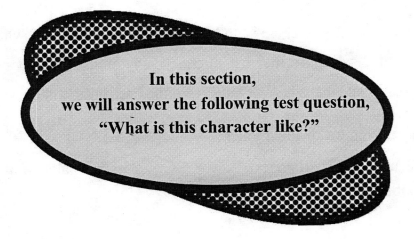

In this section,
we will answer the following test question,
"What is this character like?"

Characters, Plot, & Setting

For example, look at this description:

> Flopsy, Mopsy, and Cotton-tail, who
> were good little bunnies, went down
> the lane to gather blackberries;
>
> But Peter, who was very naughty,
> ran straight away to Mr. McGregor's
> garden, and squeezed under the gate!
>
> First he ate some lettuces and some
> French beans; and then he ate some
> radishes;
>
> And then, feeling rather sick, he
> went to look for some parsley.
>
> **–from "The Tale of Peter Rabbit"**
> **by Beatrix Potter**

How does the author describe Peter Rabbit in this passage?

   A. thin and fast   C. angry and mean

   B. allergic to lettuce   D. very hungry

Did you choose D? Good job! There is nothing in the passage that tells whether Peter is any of these things—thin, fast, angry, mean, or allergic to anything. But, it does say that Peter ate a lot of vegetables. That means he was hungry, so the best answer is D.

What judgment can you make about Peter?

   A. He doesn't like blackberries.   C. Parsley makes him sick.

   B. He disobeys his mother.   D. He is a very brave rabbit.

Chapter 13

Did you choose B? That's right! Answer A is not right. We don't know if Peter likes blackberries because the author does not tell us. We also know it's not answer C—he was looking for parsley to help him feel better. As for answer D, Peter might think he's being brave, but he's just being a bad rabbit! The passage says that Peter is very naughty. His mother tells all the children to behave, and he runs off and gets eats someone's garden. So, answer B is the best answer.

Now, try some on your own.

Practice 1: Characters

ELA3R3-e, f

Read the passage below. Choose the answer that BEST describes the character.

He walked down the street, searching up and down. He stumbled in his sneakers. They were falling apart at the seams from all the walking he was doing. He was crying a little because he was scared and tired. Where was the corner he knew? He was too frightened to ask a stranger. Where was the street that led to his house?

1. The character described in this passage is

    A. a disabled old man.   C. a lost young boy.

    B. a scared young girl.   D. a rich young man.

Billy Breeze was very kind and blew the rafts over to the island on which the Big Chestnut Tree stood. Then all the squirrels went ashore and commenced to fill their sacks with nuts, when, all of a sudden, Old Barney Owl looked out of his nest and said:

"This is my tree and these nuts belong to me. If you wish any, you must pay a penny!"

–excerpt from *Little Jack Rabbit and the Squirrel Brothers* **by David Cory**

161

2. How does the author describe Billy Breeze in this passage?

   A. nice and helpful   C. ugly and hyper

   B. slow and careful   D. fun but lazy

3. How does the author characterize Barney Owl?

   A. Barney is friendly.   C. Barney is bossy.

   B. Barney is very shy.   D. Barney is a silly owl.

PLOT—WHAT HAPPENS

What happens in a story or book is called the **plot**. The plot is the chain of events in the story. The plot is not the same all the way through—it has different parts. Every story has a beginning, middle, and end. Certain things happen at different times.

Here are the parts of the plot:

- **Introduction**—how the story starts. The author usually tells where the story is taking place and who the characters are.

    Example: Once upon a time, there was a beautiful princess. Her name was Trudy. She lived in a big castle with her father and mother, the King and the Queen.

- **Conflict**—the problem the characters face, or the journey that they have to take.

    Example: One day, Princess Trudy was in her lovely garden. Suddenly, she saw a wild wolf near the cherry tree! It saw her too and let out a low growl. Should she run? Would it attack her?

- **Rising Action**—the action in the story gets exciting.

Example: Trudy looked around and saw a sharp garden axe not far from where she stood. Maybe she could use it to defend herself! She turned and ran. She heard the wolf growl and run after her.

- **Climax**—the climax is the turning point in a story. The action of the story is at its highest, most suspenseful point.

Example: Then the wolf pounced! He knocked Trudy to the ground, inches from the axe. Then, the wolf spoke. "Princess, the ogre in the woods put a curse on me. I need a gift from you so he will remove the curse." Trudy's mind was racing—should she reach for the axe? Or should she believe the wolf? Her true nature was to be kind and gentle, so she gave the wolf an emerald ring from her finger. She was relieved when he took it and ran off.

- **Falling Action**—The action in the story slows down. The character's life settles down a bit. It may even be better.

Example: Princess Trudy recovered from the wolf attack. A week later, a brave and handsome knight came the castle. His name was Malcolm, and Trudy recognized him. He was from a neighboring kingdom. He asked the King if he could marry Princess Trudy. So, Trudy and Malcolm were engaged.

- **Resolution**—the resolution is the ending of a story. All conflict is settled.

Example: One day, in the garden, Malcolm said, "I want to thank you." Trudy replied, "What for?" He told her that he had been the one under a spell, turned into a terrible wolf. He was afraid that Trudy might kill him, or call the guards, or send the castle hounds after him. But she had given him the gift he needed for the ogre to lift the curse. "Thank you for being so gentle and trusting. I will spend the rest of my life rewarding you for your kindness."

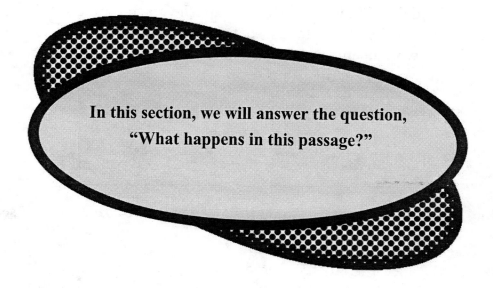

In this section, we will answer the question, "What happens in this passage?"

Practice 2: Plot

ELA3R3-e, f

Read the next story. For each section of the story, pick the part of the plot where it belongs.

A. introduction

B. conflict

C. rising action

D. climax

E. falling action

F. resolution

Chapter 13

The Crow and the Pitcher
—adapted from a fable by Aesop

There was a crow in the forest who had been wandering for days. The creek had dried up and he was very thirsty. He could not find water anywhere.

1. What part of the plot is this section? _____

The, he came upon a pitcher. Someone had left it outside, and it had filled with rainwater. But when the crow put his beak in the mouth of the pitcher, he found that only very little water was left. He could not reach to the bottom where the water was.

2. What part of the plot is this section of the story? _____

He tried, and he tried. He knew that if he did not get water, he would die of thirst. Maybe he could tip the picture…but, no, that would spill the water onto the dry ground. Maybe he could peck through the side of the picture. No, it was too hard. What to do?

3. Which part of the plot is this section? _____

Just as he was about to give up, a brilliant thought came to him. Maybe there is another way at the water! He picked up a pebble and dropped it in. Then he picked up another, and another, and dropped them in one by one. As the pebbles settled on the bottom of the pitcher, the water was rising!

4. What part of the plot is this section? _____

Finally, the water was high enough that the crow could reach it. He drank and drank. His thirst was gone. His bright idea had saved his life.

5. What part of the plot is this section of the story? _____

The crow learned a valuable lesson that day. Many times, a problem can be solved little by little, if you take the time to think about the best solution.

6. Which part of the plot is this section? _____

SETTING—WHERE AND WHEN A STORY HAPPENS

ELA3R3-e, f

The **setting** is the place and time of a story. An author can write about any time or place. The story can take place in the past, as in the time of the dinosaurs. It can happen in the present day and in a place you know well. It might be set in the future and maybe in outer space. Figuring out the setting of a passage is easy.

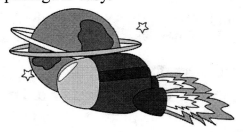

For example, look again at the story above about Princess Trudy. Where does it happen? The setting is the castle where Trudy lives. Most of the action takes place in her garden. When does it take place? Like most fairytales with magic spells, castles, a princess, and a knight, it probably happened sometime in the past.

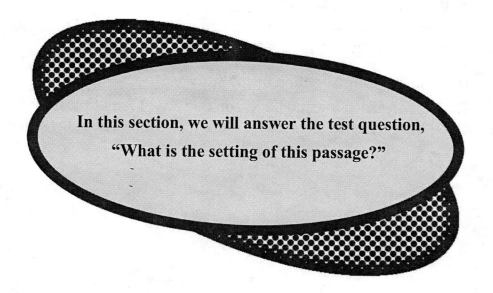

In this section, we will answer the test question, "What is the setting of this passage?"

Chapter 13

"David," said Mrs. Samson, our math teacher, "What is in your mouth?" I froze. I almost swallowed the five pieces of sour-cherry gum I had just started chewing. The sour part was just getting good. "Nothing," I mumbled around the huge ball in my mouth. My classmates laughed. I pushed the gum to the side of my cheek. "Nothing," I said again, clearer. "I don't think that lump on the side of your cheek is nothing," she replied. "Spit it out now," she commanded. I walked to the trash can and sadly spit it out, where it lay like a shining jewel. I wished I could grab it back up and eat it.

What do you think is the setting of this passage? Where and when does it happen? The setting is in a school. How do we know this? We know this because Mrs. Samson is a math teacher. Teachers work in schools. And you know that students can get in trouble for chewing gum in school! Now that you know more about setting, let's practice.

Practice 3: Setting

ELA3R3-e, f

Read the following passages. Try to figure out the setting for each one.

Building a Castle

"This will be the biggest sand castle ever!" John said. He was using a blue bucket to add more sand to the tower of the castle. "Let's put a river around it," Billy said. He took his hand and dug a trench around the base of the castle. Water came streaming in. A river now surrounded their sand castle.

1. What is the setting of this passage?

    A. in the woods.

    B. in the city.

    C. at the beach.

    D. on a mountain.

If you chose C, you're right! The passage takes place at the beach. Now try some on your own.

Characters, Plot, & Setting

Summer Ball

It was hot. All of my teammates were sweating. The field buzzed with flies and bees. My mom waved to me from the bench. "Come on, Carlos, hit a home run!" she shouted. The pitcher wound his arm and threw the ball. I didn't take my eyes off the ball. I swung. The bat hit the ball, and I ran like mad to first base.

2. Where does this passage take place?
   A. inside a tent
   B. at a baseball field
   C. in a soccer field
   D. inside Carlos's house

Camping

It was cool the morning they drove off. Everything they needed for the camping trip was loaded into the back of the truck: A tent, sleeping bags, flashlights and some food. Jason's dad drove carefully. The road was curvy. The truck climbed slowly up the mountain. They had been driving for three hours. Jason looked at his dad and asked, "How much longer?"

3. Where does this passage take place?
   A. in the woods
   B. in a basement
   C. in a plane
   D. on a lake

Monster River

The river was a monster. It pushed us further downstream. We were never supposed to go this far. We jumped over the edge of the raft long ago, holding onto the edge with our hands. We tried to slow the raft with our feet. But it didn't work. Our feet just slipped over hard rocks. The icy water crept through our clothing and pierced into our skin like claws. The current was getting stronger. We knew the river well enough. Up ahead was a waterfall.

Not a very large waterfall, but still a good drop. We didn't say it, but we both knew we'd go over.

4. Where does this passage take place?

A. in a house

B. on a river

C. in an ocean

D. in the desert

CHAPTER 13 SUMMARY

- **Characterization**—how an author writes about characters to make them "real" to readers. An author can use **description** to tell about a character. He can also use **dialogue** to show how a character talks to others.

- **Plot**—the events that happen at the beginning, middle, and end of a story. The plot has several parts. These are **introduction**, **conflict**, **rising action**, **climax**, **falling action**, and **resolution**.

- **Setting**—where and when a story happens.

LET'S REVIEW

ELA3R3-e, f

Read the following passages and answer the questions.

—excerpt from *Peter Pan* by James M. Barrie

For a moment after Mr. and Mrs. Darling left the house the night-lights by the beds of the three children continued to burn clearly. They were awfully nice little night-lights, and one cannot help wishing that they could have kept awake to see Peter; but Wendy's light blinked and gave such a yawn that the other two yawned also, and before they could close their mouths all the three went out.

There was another light in the room now, a thousand times brighter than the night-lights, and in the time we have taken to say this, it has been in all the drawers in the nursery, looking for Peter's shadow, rummaged the wardrobe and turned every pocket inside out. It was not really a light; it made this light by flashing about so quickly, but when it came to rest for a second you saw it was a fairy, no longer than your hand, but still growing.

It was a girl called Tinker Bell exquisitely gowned in a skeleton leaf, cut low and square, through which her figure could be seen to the best advantage. She was slightly inclined to embonpoint [plumpness].

A moment after the fairy's entrance the window was blown open by the breathing of the little stars, and Peter dropped in. He had carried Tinker Bell part of the way, and his hand was still messy with the fairy dust.

"Tinker Bell," he called softly, after making sure that the children were asleep. "Tink, where are you?" She was in a jug for the moment, and liking it extremely; she had never been in a jug before.

"Oh, do come out of that jug, and tell me, do you know where they put my shadow?"

Chapter 13

1. What is the setting of this passage?

   A. the woods on a winter evening

   B. a big kitchen with many cabinets

   C. the playroom of a fairy castle

   D. a children's bedroom at night

2. The author describes Tinker Bell as
   A. slightly deaf.   C. rather ugly.
   B. very fast.   D. stuck up.

3. The first paragraph is the introduction of this chapter of the story. The author uses it to introduce
   A. what will happen in other chapters.   C. the characters and the setting.
   B. just the little fairy, Tinker Bell.   D. only Mr. and Mrs. Darling.

4. What conflict is mentioned in this part of the story?

   A. Peter Pan and Tinker Bell are searching for Peter's shadow.

   B. The children are having trouble staying awake to play with Peter.

   C. Tinker Bell has lost her skeleton-leaf dress in the children's room.

   D. Mr. and Mrs. Darling may come back soon and catch Peter and Tinker.

The Emperor's New Clothes
–adapted from the story by Hans Christian Andersen

Many years ago, there was an Emperor. He loved new clothes so much that he spent all his money on them. He had a different suit for each hour of the day.

One day, two thieves, disguised as tailors, came to the city. They told people that they could make beautiful clothes of the finest material. The colors were bright and the patterns were amazing. But these clothes were invisible to anyone who was not worthy. If a person was unfit for the office he held, or was dull or stupid in any way, he would not be able to see the clothes.

"These must, indeed, be splendid clothes!" thought the Emperor. "If I have such a suit, I can find out who in my realms is unfit for his office. I would also be able to tell the wise from the foolish! I must have these clothes immediately." And he paid the two men so they could begin work.

The two pretend tailors pretended to work very hard. In reality, they did nothing at all. They asked for the most delicate silk and the purest gold thread. They put both into their own knapsacks, and then continued their pretend work until late at night.

The Emperor wanted to know how the work was coming. He thought about who to send. After all, a simpleton or someone unfit for his job would not be able to see the fine cloth!

"I will send my faithful old minister," said the Emperor at last. "He will see how the cloth looks; for he is a man of sense, and no one can be more suitable for his office than he is."

So the faithful old minister went to the room where the pretend tailors were pretend working. He saw them working on nothing.

"What is the meaning of this?" he thought. "I cannot see the least bit of cloth." However, he did not say his thoughts aloud. "I will never confess that I could not see the stuff." So he told the thieves their work was excellent and that he would describe it to the Emperor.

The minister told the Emperor about the fine fabric and lovely patterns. In the next few days, the Emperor sent more officers of his court to look the work. They all came back with glowing reports. None of them wanted to be fired or called stupid!

Finally, the day came when the Emperor would wear the new clothes in a great parade through the city. The pretend tailors stayed up the whole night pretending to finish the clothes. As the sun came up, they shouted, "The Emperor's new clothes are ready!"

Now the Emperor, with all his court, came to the tailors. They raised their arms, as if holding something up, and said, "Here are your Majesty's trousers! Here is the scarf! Here is the shirt! The whole suit is as light as a cobweb. One might think one has nothing at all on—that is the great quality of this delicate cloth."

They pretended to dress the Emperor. Then he looked in the big mirror, while they praised how wonderful he looked. All the lords and ladies of the court pretended, too, as no one wanted to be called simple or unfit for office.

So now the Emperor walked in the parade through the streets of his capital. All the people standing by, and those at the windows, cried out, "Oh! How beautiful are our Emperor's new clothes! How graceful and lovely the fabric is!" In short, no one would allow that he could not see the clothes.

"But the Emperor has nothing at all on!" said a little child.

"Listen to the voice of innocence!" said his father. What the boy had said was whispered from one to another.

"But he has nothing at all on!" at last cried out all the people. The Emperor was upset. He knew that the people were right.

5. What judgment can you make about the Emperor?
   A. He eats so much his clothes don't fit.
   B. He loves clothes more than anything.
   C. He gives many gifts to all his people.
   D. He likes and trusts everyone in his court.

6. Which of the following is the climax of the passage?
   A. when the thieves come to town pretending to be tailors
   B. when the Emperor decides he must have a new suit
   C. when the minister goes to see how the tailors are doing
   D. when the child shouts that the Emperor has no clothes

7. How does the author characterize all the people in the court and the city?
   A. Their most important value is to always tell the truth.
   B. The people love the Emperor and don't want to upset him.
   C. They care most about what other people think of them.
   D. No one has seen such beautiful clothes, so they are excited.

8. What is the setting of this passage?

   A. the capital city of an empire, in the past

   B. a small village, sometime in the recent past

   C. a big city in America, in the near future

   D. backstage at the performance of a play

9. Before the parade, the Emperor sends different people to inspect the fake clothes. Then he tries them on and also pretends to see them. All of these events leading up to the parade are an example of what part of the plot?

   A. introduction

   B. rising action

   C. climax

   D. falling action

10. What is the resolution (ending) in the plot of this story?

   A. Everyone shouts, "But he has nothing at all on!"

   B. The thieves escape from the city with all the things they stole.

   C. The Emperor realizes that he has been fooled and has no clothes on.

   D. The little boy is taken to jail by the court guards for revealing the truth.

Chapter 14
Finding Information in Graphics

This chapter covers Georgia standard

ELA3R3-h	Interprets information from illustrations, diagrams, charts, graphs, and graphic organizers.

FINDING INFORMATION IN GRAPHICS

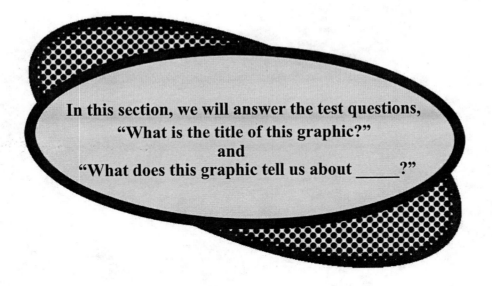

In this section, we will answer the test questions,
"What is the title of this graphic?"
and
"What does this graphic tell us about _____?"

A **graphic** is a picture or a drawing. A graphic can be a chart or an illustration like a cartoon. Usually graphics give information in picture form. Rather than reading, you have to look at the pictures to find the information you need to answer the questions.

Finding Information in Graphics

Some common graphics that go with articles and stories include:

- photographs
- tables
- line graphs
- drawings
- pie charts
- diagrams

For example, look at the two graphics below. Both show the same information. But they show it in different ways.

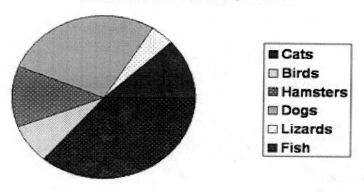

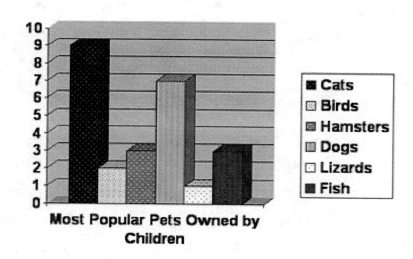

Chapter 14

Practice 1:   Finding information in Graphics

ELA3R3-h

Look at the following graphics and answer the questions that follow. The first one has been done for you.

The pie graph below gives information about two pizza places. The graphs compare different pizza crusts and how many are sold.

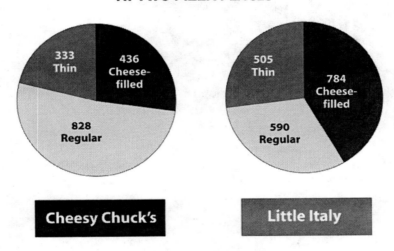

**KINDS OF CRUSTS ORDERED
AT TWO PIZZA PLACES**

333 Thin 436 Cheese-filled 828 Regular

Cheesy Chuck's

505 Thin 784 Cheese-filled 590 Regular

Little Italy

1. How many regular crusts were ordered at Cheesy Chuck's?

    A. 333   B. 828   C. 590   D. none

Did you choose answer B? You're right! The graph of Cheesy Chuck's tells us the exact number of regular crusts ordered. All you have to do is look at the graph to find the answer. Good work. Now try the next few on your own.

2. What kind of crust is ordered the MOST at Little Italy?
    A. thin crust
    B. regular crust
    C. cheese-filled crust
    D. no crust

3. What kind of crust is ordered the LEAST at Cheesy Chuck's?
   A. thin crust
   B. cheese-filled crust
   C. no crust
   D. regular crust

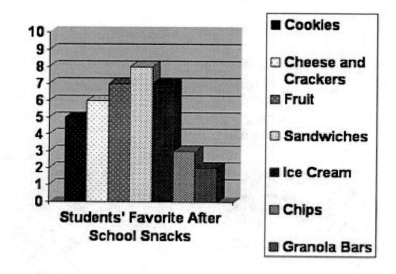

4. What is the title of this graph?
   A. After School Snacks
   B. Students' Favorite
   C. Students' Favorite After School Snacks
   D. Bar Graph

5. What is the MOST popular after school snack?
   A. cookies   B. ice cream   C. granola bars   D. sandwiches

6. What is the LEAST popular after school snack?
   A. sandwiches
   B. fruit
   C. cheese and crackers
   D. granola bars

CHAPTER 14 SUMMARY

- **Graphic**—a picture or a drawing. A graphic can be a chart, a photograph, a graph, or an illustration like a cartoon.

- **Finding Information in Graphics**—graphics usually give information in picture form. Rather than reading, you have to look at the pictures to find the information you need.

LET'S REVIEW

ELA3R3-h

Look at the tables that follow and answer the questions.

Favorite Things to Do After School- Ms. Johnson's Third Grade Class

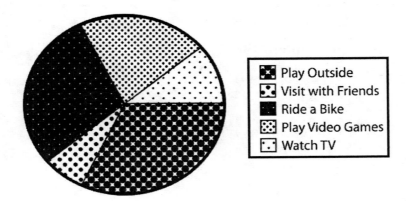

1. What is the title of this graph?

   A. Playing Outside, by Ms. Johnson's Third Grade Class

   B. Favorite Things to Do After School—Ms. Johnson's Third Grade Class

   C. Visiting with Friends and Other Fun Things to Do after School

   D. Ms. Johnson's Third Grade Class Tells What to Do for Fun after School

2. What is the MOST popular thing to do after school?
   A. play video games
   B. watch TV
   C. ride a bike
   D. play outside

3. What is the LEAST popular thing to do after school?
   A. ride a bike
   B. play video games
   C. talk on the phone
   D. play outside

Toy Inventions
1880 - 1982

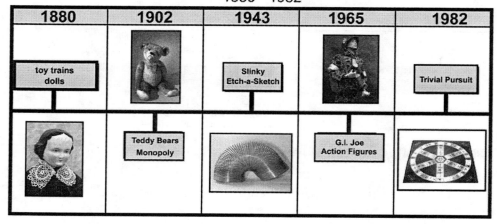

4. What is the title of this timeline?
   A. Teddy Bears
   B. Dolls
   C. 1880
   D. Toy Inventions

5. What years does this timeline cover?
   A. 1902
   B. 1965
   C. 1943 to 1965
   D. 1880 to 1982

6. What toys were invented in 1943?
   A. toy trains and Trivial Pursuit
   B. the Slinky and Etch-a-Sketch
   C. Monopoly and the Teddy Bear
   D. Trivial Pursuit and G. I. Joe

7. When were Teddy Bears invented?
   A. 1943
   B. 1902
   C. 1982
   D. 1880

Mastering the Georgia 3rd Grade CRCT in Reading
Practice Test 1

The purpose of this practice test is to measure your knowledge in reading comprehension. This practice test is based on the Georgia Performance Standards for reading and adheres to the sample question format provided by the Georgia Department of Education.

General Directions:

1. Read all directions carefully.

2. Read each question or sample. Then choose the best answer.

3. Choose only one answer for each question. If you change an answer, be sure to erase your original answer completely.

Practice Test 1

Read the passage. Answer the questions after it.

Summer Vacation

Every year, we go to Myrtle Beach for a whole week. It is the best place on Earth. During high season, Myrtle Beach was ranked the fifth most popular beach in the United States in 2007. The Atlantic Ocean is a gorgeous blue and the waves are sometimes rough. My family has been going to the beach since I was born. When I was a baby, I would crawl in the waves. Once, I got swept away by a big wave. I was not even scared, but my mom sure was. "Sammy! You come back here," she cried out. She saved me.

I like to build sand castles right on the edge of the sea. People come from all over to enjoy the wide beaches, the Atlantic Ocean, and an incredible range of activities, entertainment, golf, shopping, and dining. I like the amusement park because they have four fast roller coasters.

On the beach, I like to collect seashells, especially the conch shells. Digging in the sand is another favorite activity that I enjoy with my brother, Kenny. We race each other to see who can dig the biggest hole. I love the feeling of the wind in my hair and the sun on my back.

1. Sammy likes to build sand castles near the _____.

   A. sea   B. see

   3R2C

2. What kinds of seashells does Sammy enjoy collecting?

   A. clam shells

   B. conch shells

   C. tri-colored shells

   D. starfish

   3R3J

3. Where does this story take place?

   A. on a beach   C. in a forest

   B. at an amusement park   D. on a boat on the ocean

   3R3E

4. On the beach, which activity have Sammy and Kenny not tried yet?   3R3J
   A. building sand castles   C. picking up rocks
   B. digging holes   D. looking for seashells

Look at this table, and then answer the questions that follow.

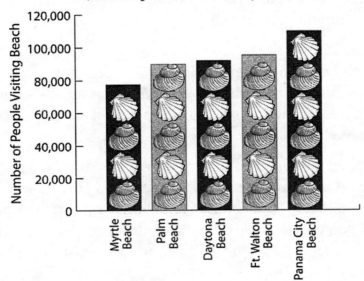

Most Popular Beaches in the United States
(Based on high season from March-September, 2007)

5. Which beach was the most popular in 2007?   3R3H
   A. Panama City Beach   C. Myrtle Beach
   B. Daytona Beach   D. Palm Beach

6. Which beach came in fourth place for being the most popular beach?   3R3H
   A. Myrtle Beach   C. Daytona Beach
   B. Palm Beach   D. Ft. Walton

7. Which beach came in second place for being the most popular beach?   3R3H
   A. Myrtle Beach   C. Daytona Beach
   B. Palm Beach   D. Ft. Walton

Read the passage, and then answer the questions.

How Brother Rabbit Tricked Wally Whale and Eddy Elephant

An African-American Folktale

Long ago, Brother Rabbit was running along on the sand when he saw Wally Whale and Eddy Elephant at the water's edge. Brother Rabbit snuck behind a tree to listen to what was being said. The sun was rising and looked like a giant glowing beach ball.

"You are the strongest thing on the land, Eddy Elephant," said Wally Whale, "and I am the strongest thing in the sea. If we join together, we can rule all the animals on Earth." "Very good, very good," trumpeted Elephant. "That suits me. We will do it." Brother Rabbit snickered to himself, "They won't rule me."

He hopped away and got a very long, thick rope, and he got his big drum. He put the drum behind the tree where he had been hiding. Brother Rabbit headed out to trick Wally and Eddy. "Oh, please, dear strong Mr. Whale," he said, "will you do me a favor? My cow is stuck in the mud just down the beach from here. And I can't pull her out. You are so strong and so kind. Will you please help me?"

Whale was so pleased with the compliment that at once he said, "Yes." "OK," said Rabbit, "I will tie this end of my thick rope to you, and I will run away and tie the other end round my cow, and when I am ready I will beat my big drum. When you hear that, pull very, very hard, for the cow is stuck very deep in the mud." Brother Rabbit tied the rope end to Whale, and hopped off looking for Eddy Elephant. Brother Rabbit was giggling and laughing, and laughing and giggling.

"Oh, please, powerful Elephant," he said, "will you do me a favor?"

"What is it?" asked Elephant. "My cow is stuck in the mud about a quarter of a mile from here," said little Brother Rabbit, "and I cannot pull her out. Of course, you could. Won't you please help me?" "Certainly," said Elephant grandly. Eddy Elephant was proud that Brother Rabbit asked him for his help. "Then," said Brother Rabbit, "I will tie one end of this thick rope to your trunk and the other to my cow, and as soon as I have tied her tightly I will beat my big drum. When you hear the drum, pull as hard as you can, for my cow is very heavy." "Not to worry," said Elephant, "I could pull thirty-three cows." "I am sure you could," said Rabbit politely. "Pull gently at first so as not to scare her into fright," cautioned Brother Rabbit. "Not to worry," said Elephant. Brother Rabbit was giggling and laughing, and laughing and giggling.

Then Brother Rabbit tied the end of the rope tightly round Eddy Elephant's trunk and ran away into the bushes. Brother Rabbit smiled as he sat down to beat his big drum behind the tree. Wally began to pull, and Eddy began to pull, and in a jiffy the rope was stretched tight.

"This is a very heavy cow," said Elephant, "but I'll get her!" And he gave a tremendous pull digging his feet into the firm soil. "Dear me!" said Whale. "That cow must be stuck mighty tight," and he drove his tail deep in the water and gave a mighty pull.

Wally Whale pulled harder. Eddy Elephant pulled harder. Pretty soon Whale found himself sliding toward the land. The reason was each time Elephant pulled the rope in a little, he took a turn with it around his trunk! But when Whale found himself sliding toward the land, he was so angry with the cow that he dove head first down to the bottom of the sea. And what a pull that was! Brother Rabbit was giggling and laughing, and laughing and giggling. Elephant was jerked off his feet, and came slipping and sliding to the beach and into the surf. He was terribly angry. He braced himself with all his might and pulled his best. At the pull Whale came up out of the water.

"Who is pulling me?" said Wally Whale.

"Who is pulling me?" trumpeted Eddy Elephant.

And then they could see that the rope was tightly tied around each of them. "I'll teach you to play cow!" roared Elephant. "I'll show you not to mess with me!" fumed Whale. And they began to pull again, but this time the thick rope broke. Wally Whale turned a back flip and Eddy Elephant fell over backwards. At that, they were both so ashamed that neither would speak to the other. So that broke the deal between Wally and Eddy. And again, Brother Rabbit sat in the bushes and was giggling and laughing, and laughing and giggling.

8. Why did the author write this passage?   3R3P
    A. to inform people about rescuing cows
    B. to persuade people that elephants are strong
    C. to educate people about how tricky rabbits are
    D. to entertain people with an amusing story

9. Why was Brother Rabbit giggling and laughing, and laughing and giggling?   3R3L
    A. He thought that Wally Whale looked funny.
    B. He thought that Eddy Elephant looked funny.
    C. His drum made a funny sound.
    D. He knew he tricked Wally Whale and Eddy Elephant.

10. Name a word that is a synonym for *fumed*, used in the last paragraph.   3R2C
    A. sweet   B. gentle   C. angry   D. disappointed

11. What kind of instrument did Brother Rabbit use?   3R3J
    A. violin   B. tambourine   C. clarinet   D. drum

12. What genre is the passage "How Brother Rabbit Tricked Wally Whale and   3R3N
    Eddy Elephant"?
    A. nonfiction   C. science fiction
    B. fiction   D. history

13. What will MOST LIKELY happen next in the story?   3R3B
    A. The Whale and Elephant will think they got the cow out.
    B. The Whale and Elephant will not try to rule other animals.
    C. All the characters will discuss the uses for thick ropes.
    D. Brother Rabbit will teach the Whale and Elephant how to play the drum.

14. Who did Brother Rabbit first visit with the rope in this story?   3R3E
    A. Eddy Elephant   C. Wally Whale
    B. Brother Bear   D. Willie Whale

15. Where does this story take place?   3R3E, F
    A. Asia   B. Australia   C. Africa   D. Antarctica

Read this passage. Answer the questions after it.

Grandma Georgiana

My grandma is a sweet lady. She bakes bread on the weekends for breakfast. She dresses very plain, wearing navy pants and a white top.

She is pretty with smooth caramel-colored skin and large brown eyes. She has a tender expression and a warm smile.

I do not want to go to school today. I want to stay at home with Grandma Georgiana and work in her garden. She has many kinds of flowers and vegetables. Grandma Georgiana grows watermelons, peas, beans, and tomatoes. Last week, one tomato plant grew fourteen tomatoes.

She shares the vegetables and flowers from her garden with her neighbors.

Grandma Georgiana also walks two miles every day. She takes her dog, Little Bit, along with her. Little Bit is a teacup pup because he only weighs two pounds and he can fit inside a teacup. Have you ever seen such a tiny dog? While she's walking, she takes a small plastic bag and picks up garbage from the side of the road. She is a good citizen and she tries to help her family and friends all the time. I love my Grandma Georgiana.

16. The OPPOSITE of the word *sweet* is   3R2C
    A. kind   B. mean   C. nice   D. light

17. Which statement is MOST LIKELY an opinion of the author?   3R3D
    A. Grandma Georgiana plants flowers and vegetables.
    B. She walks two miles every day.
    C. Grandma Georgiana likes her garden.
    D. Grandma Georgiana owns a tiny dog that weighs two pounds.

18. My grandma bakes _____ every Sunday morning for breakfast.   3R2C
    A. bred   B. bread

19. The OPPOSITE of the word *plain* is   3R2C
    A. boring   B. simple   C. fancy   D. ordinary

20. The OPPOSITE of the word *pretty* is   3R2C
    A. beautiful   B. cute   C. ugly   D. plain

21. Have you ever seen such a *tiny* dog?

    What is a synonym for the word *tiny*?

    A. little   B. gigantic   C. medium   D. big

22. What is the BEST summary of this passage?
    A. Grandma Georgiana's garden
    B. a story about Little Bit
    C. the life of Grandma Georgiana
    D. how to make Grandma Georgiana's bread

Read this passage. Answer the questions that follow.

Rainy Days

by Anonymous

Rainy days are sometimes gray
But birds and squirrels still come out to play **2**

Mister Sun hides his face in the clouds
And it's fun to curl up and read aloud   **4**

Sunny days are made for wild outside fun
But I also like to be calm and quiet   **6**
      when there is no sun.

23. What genre of writing is this?
    A. drama   C. fairytald
    B. poetry   D. autobiography

24. What can you infer about the person who wrote this?
    A. The author likes both sunny and rainy days.
    B. The author hates rainy days.
    C. The author likes to read.
    D. The author likes birds and squirrels.

25. Which lines rhyme? 3R3N
    A. lines 1 and 3   B. lines 1 and 2   C. lines 3 and 4   D. both B and C

_____

26. What is the **root** of the word *settler*? 3R2E
    A. set   B. sett   C. settle   D. er

27. What the **suffix** in the word *settler* mean? 3R2E
    A. without   C. in the manner of
    B. full of or having   D. someone who does something

28. Choose the word that means both "put it down" and "a collection." 3R2B
    A. sit   B. set   C. bring   D. brang

Read the passage, and then answer the question about it.

Lonny was going too fast down the hill on his new skateboard. He knew he couldn't make the turn, and Mr. Hamish's fence was straight ahead. He was so glad he was wearing his helmet and all his protective pads!

29. What will MOST LIKELY happen next? 3R3B
    A. Lonny will come to a complete stop.
    B. Lonny will make the turn successfully.
    C. Lonny will crash into Mr. Hamish's fence.
    D. Lonny will stop riding his skateboard for good.

30. The girls began to *snicker* during the Teddy Bear Tea Party. When the parents 3R2F
    heard the giggling, they smiled at each other. The Teddy Bears were quiet.
    What does *snicker* probably mean?
    A. sleepy   B. angry   C. laugh   D. cry

31. Add the prefix un- to the word *lucky*. It makes a new word, which means 3R2E
    A. to be really lucky   C. not lucky
    B. safe   D. dangerous

Practice Test 1

Read this passage, and answer the questions after it.

Tyler's Room

My mom walked in my room and squeezed her nose tight with her right hand. "Tyler! What is that smell?" My room was messy. My room has always been messy. My mom teases me that even my crib was messy when I was a baby. There were baseball cards, marbles, and dirty clothes on the floor. My bed was not made, my books were not categorized on my shelves, and the dust bunnies were having a party under my bed. Yes, it was a mess. My mom handed me a trash bag and a laundry basket. "Clean this up this instant," she stated firmly. It was a sad day in my room. When I finished cleaning my room, I hit the hay because I was so tired.

32. What genre is the passage "Tyler's Room"?   3R3N
    A. advertisement   B. fiction   C. drama   D. poetry

33. Why is Tyler's mom MOST LIKELY holding her nose?   3R3F
    A. She is about to sneeze.
    B. She doesn't want to see the mess.
    C. Tyler's dirty clothes smell bad.
    D. Tyler asked her to go swimming.

34. The word *categorized* means   3R2F
    A. stacked.   C. organized.
    B. thrown.   D. discarded.

35. Which of these happened last in the story?   3R3E, J
    A. Tyler's mom gave him a trash bag and a laundry basket
    B. The mom walked into Tyler's bedroom
    C. There was a dust bunny party under the bed
    D. Tyler vacuumed the carpet

36. What was NOT on the floor of Tyler's room?   3R3J
    A. baseball cards   C. marbles
    B. action figures   D. dirty clothes

37. A homograph has the same spelling but the word has two different meanings. 3R2C
What means "to go away" or "parts of trees that fall down"?
   A. leaves   B. leaf   C. left   D. fell down

Read the passage. Answer the questions that follow.

Tamara Gets a Dog

Tamara decided to buy a dog for the first time after being a cat lover for many years. First, she went to a dog show to look at different kinds of dogs. The people at the dog show recommended several types of dogs, including chows, shepherds, terriers, and boxers. Then Tamara went to several pet stores and asked for more information about each type of dog that she liked. After much thought, Tamara chose a mutt from the local Humane Society.

On the way home, Tamara and her new dog went shopping. She purchased a large bed, several chew toys, a red collar, a red leash, and some food. Within the first week, Tamara took her dog, Charlie, to a veterinarian for a check-up. Charlie had to get three shots. He was not happy. Tamara and Charlie were becoming fast friends.

Charlie was learning how to go to the bathroom outside, but sometimes he had accidents on Tamara's new white carpet. He liked to chew on her shoes which became a big problem. Charlie also liked to chase cats in the neighborhood and Tamara had to leave him on his leash at all times. She decided to enroll him in obedience school to improve his behavior. On the last day of dog training school, Charlie won an award for good behavior.

38. Which word is a homophone for *week*? 3R2C
   A. leak   B. weed   C. weak   D. wake

39. Which word is a synonym for *within*? 3R2C
   A. inside   B. outside   C. around   D. down

40. In deciding what kind of dog to buy, what did Tamara do first? 3R3M
   A. She visited pet stores.
   B. She went to a dog show.
   C. She talked to dog trainers.
   D. She asked for information about dogs.

41. What kind of dog did Tamara choose?   3R3M
    A. a chow   B. a shepherd   C. a mutt   D. a boxer

42. What did Tamara purchase at the pet store?   3R3M
    A. some food and a chew toy
    B. a bed, a collar and leash, food, toys
    C. a red collar and matching leash
    D. a bed, a collar, and some food

43. Why did Charlie have to go to obedience school?   3R3L
    A. He needed to learn how to fetch and to sit.
    B. He had to learn to go to the bathroom outside.
    C. He wanted to win an award.
    D. He had to learn to behave.

44. Which of the following BEST describes how Tamara and Charlie feel at the   3R3F
    end of the passage?
    A. angry   B. sad   C. happy   D. lonely

Read the passage, and then answer the questions.

Diggin' Up Fossils

Dinosaurs roamed the Earth millions of years ago. How do we know so much about these prehistoric animals and plant life from so long ago? How can we find out about this time in history when no humans were present on Earth? The answer lies in the ground. What we have learned comes from the remains of dead plants and animals called fossils. People that study the history of life by investigating fossils are called paleontologists.

These remains that have hardened and turned to stone are called fossils. Fossils are rocks that contain the imprint of bones, shells, or leaves. Not every plant or animal becomes a fossil when it dies. Some dry up under the sun or they are blown away by strong winds.

Becoming a fossil is a lengthy process. When a plant or an animal dies, everything has to be just right to make a fossil. Sand or mud has to cover the animal or plant quickly. That way, neither the wind nor the sun can damage it. Over time, the fossil is formed and preserved. To find a fossil, paleontologists dig deep into the ground in areas where fossils have been known to be found. They might find a bone, a tooth, or a part of a leaf. If they are lucky, they sometimes find a footprint of a dinosaur. Every fossil gives us more information about life in prehistoric times.

Millions of fossils have been found. If you think about all of the museums, university paleontology labs, and private collectors, there really are a lot of fossils that have been discovered!

However when you think of the billions and billions of living things that have inhabited the Earth over the last 550 million years, only a very small percentage are immortalized in stone! You might want to buy one or find a fossil of your own.

45. The word *imprint* from the second paragraph means   3R2F
    A. enlarge.   B. dinosaur.   C. shape.   D. thumbprint.

46. What is the main idea of this passage?   3R3J
    A. careers in paleontology
    B. investigating fossils from prehistoric times
    C. learning more about how petroleum fuel is made
    D. finding your own fossil

47. Which of the following statements is a fact?   3R3D
    A. Dinosaurs roamed the Earth millions of years ago.
    B. Fossils are fun to collect and look at.
    C. Paleontologists work harder than other scientists.
    D. Fossils are really easy to find in the crust of the Earth.

48. What are fossils? 3R3M
    A. mud or sand from prehistoric times
    B. dinosaur teeth
    C. the remains of dead plants and animals
    D. paper that has decomposed

49. Why do we study fossils? 3R3L, M
    A. to learn about dinosaur teeth
    B. to study the history of Earth before humans
    C. to learn how paper decomposes
    D. to educate readers about paleontologists

50. Which word contains a prefix that means *before*? 3R2E
    A. unstable   B. prehistoric   C. dislike   D. incline

Mastering the Georgia 3rd Grade CRCT in Reading
Practice Test 2

The purpose of this practice test is to measure your knowledge in reading comprehension. This practice test is based on the Georgia Performance Standards for reading and adheres to the sample question format provided by the Georgia Department of Education.

General Directions:

1. Read all directions carefully.

2. Read each question or sample. Then choose the best answer.

3. Choose only one answer for each question. If you change an answer, be sure to erase your original answer completely.

Practice Test 2

1. When will you _____ at school?

   A. bee   B. bea   C. be

2. A large furry animal that lives in the woods is called a

   A. bear.   B. bare.   C. barre.

   3R2C

3. Which of these words is a root word with no prefixes of suffixes?

   A. division

   B. multiplication

   C. add

   D. subtract

   3R2E

Read this passage. Then, answer the questions about it.

The Town Mouse and the City Mouse
Adapted from a story by Aesop

Now you must know that once upon a time, Town Mouse went to visit his cousin who lived in the country. The Country Mouse was excited to see his cousin and he made him feel very welcome. Beans, bacon, cheese, and bread, were all Country Mouse had to offer, but he offered them freely.

The Town Mouse stuck up his pink nose at the country food. He said, "I cannot understand, cousin, how you can put up with such poor food as this. Of course you cannot expect anything better in the country. You should come with me and I will show you how to live. When you have been in town a week, you will wonder why you chose a country life."

So the Country Mouse agreed to stay with his cousin in town. "You will want some food after our long trip," said the polite Town Mouse, and he took his friend into the grand dining room. They snuck in through a mouse hole near the front hall of the large home. There they found the remains of a fine feast. There were left over roast rinds, cheese nibbles, and crusts of bread. It was a delicious meal. Then they found the dessert table complete with bits of chocolate éclairs, oatmeal raisin cookies, and fruit tarts.

Suddenly they heard growling and barking. "What is that?" said the Country Mouse. "It is only the dogs of the house," answered Town Mouse.

"Only!" said the Country Mouse. "I do not like that music at my dinner." Just at that moment the door flew open, and two huge guard dogs ran in, and the two mice scampered away.

"Good-bye, cousin," said the Country Mouse. "What! Going so soon?" said the Town Mouse. "Yes," replied Country Mouse, "Better beans and bacon in peace than cakes and meat in fear."

4. The passage "The Town Mouse and the City Mouse" is   3R3N
   A. letter.   B. a folktale.   C. a fable.   D. nonfiction.

5. Which word from the passage means the OPPOSITE of *peace*?   3R2C
   A. smooth   B. rough   C. war   D. whole

6. How did the Country Mouse feel when he heard the dogs barking?   3R3F, L
   A. scared   B. excited   C. sad   D. lonely

7. Why does the Country Mouse decide to go home?   3R3F, L
   A. He wants to live in peace without being afraid.
   B. He prefers beans and bacon to the fine feast.
   C. He does not like his cousin.
   D. He likes the sound of crickets at night.

8. Which sentence BEST explains why the Town Mouse was unhappy in the   3R3L
   country?
   A. He stuck up his pink nose at the country food.
   B. He did not like to sleep in the woods.
   C. He was homesick.
   D. He complained it was too far away.

9. In paragraph 4 of the passage, what does *scampered* mean?   3R2F
   A. to walk slowly   C. to dance
   B. to run quickly   D. to smile

Read the passage, and then answer the questions after it.

The Milky Way Galaxy

The Milky Way is not just a candy bar! It is an enormous spiral galaxy that includes the Sun and its solar system, including Earth. Its name comes from its appearance as a faintly luminous band that stretches across the Earth's sky at night. The hazy appearance is from the combined light of stars that are too far away to be seen without a powerful telescope. The band looks like a misty veil and includes some 200 billion stars and massive amounts of dust clouds and gas atoms. The individual stars that can be seen in the sky are those in the Milky Way Galaxy that lie closer to the solar system. They can be seen without a telescope, like the North Star and the Big Dipper.

The Milky Way Galaxy contains both the young, brilliant blue, so-called type I stars; and the older, giant red, type II stars. The central area of the Milky Way has mostly type II stars. Some astronomers believe that in the center of the Milky Way is a gigantic black hole. Much of the Milky Way is filled with interstellar dust and gas.

If you were looking down on the Milky Way Galaxy, it would look like a large pinwheel rotating in space. It is believed that the Milky Way is 14 billion years old!

10. What is the author's MAIN purpose for writing this passage?   3R3P
    A. to ask people to stop polluting
    B. to educate readers about the Milky Way Galaxy
    C. to educate readers about red stars and blue stars
    D. to entertain readers about black holes

11. The Milky Way Galaxy is defined as a _____ galaxy.   3R3M
    A. rectangular   B. black   C. spiral   D. band

12. Which word is an antonym for *luminous*?   3R2C
    A. bright   B. shiny   C. plain   D. dull

13. How many stars do astronomers believe are in the Milky Way Galaxy?   3R3M
    A. 200 million   B. 200 billion   C. 14 million   D. 14 billion

14. Which statement is a fact and not an opinion?   3R3D
    A. The Milky Way Galaxy is pretty.
    B. The Sun and Earth are in the Milky Way Galaxy.
    C. Astronomers have a difficult job.
    D. People need to take care of the Earth every day.

15. The author describes the Milky Way Galaxy as   3R3J
    A. an area that is milk white in the sky.
    B. a pinwheel that moves fast.
    C. a faintly luminous band.
    D. a large collection of stars.

Read the passage. Then, answer the questions that follow.

Why the Sea is Salty

One winter long ago, there were two brothers named Ted and Tony. Ted was rich, and Tony was poor. The rich brother was stingy and lived in a great house. The wind howled outside, and the snow almost covered the tiny shack in which the poor brother lived. "We cannot starve," said Tony to his wife. "I will ask my brother, Ted, to help us."

It annoyed the rich brother to have the poor brother ask for help. The rich brother said angrily, "Here, take this meat and go to the dwarfs. They will boil it for you." So the poor brother left in search of the dwarfs. He trudged slowly through the snow until he saw five dwarfs and went to their home.

It certainly was a peculiar place! The Chief Dwarf spotted Tony and said, "Ho, ho! Who enters our cave?" The dwarfs were teasing him and picking at the meat in Tony's hands. They wanted the meat for their supper. "What will you give me for the meat?" asked the poor brother. "We have no gold," said the dwarfs, "but we will give you the mill that stands behind the door."

"Why do I want a mill?" cried Tony. "I am hungry and have come to cook the meat for me and my wife," said the poor brother. "It is a wonderful mill," the Chief Dwarf replied. "It will grind anything in the world that you might wish, except snow and meat. I will show you how to use it." So the poor brother agreed, and he gave them the meat and took the mill.

The Chief Dwarf said, "When you wish the mill to grind, use these words:

Grind, quickly grind, little mill,
Grind–with a right good will!"

When you wish the mill to stop grinding, you must say, "Halt, halt, little mill! The mill will obey you," stated the Chief Dwarf. Taking the little mill under his arm, the poor brother climbed up the hill, through the snow, until he reached his shack. When he arrived in front of the shack, he put the little mill down on the snow, and said at once,

"Grind, quickly grind, little mill,

Grind a HOUSE—with a right good will!"

The little mill ground and ground until there stood, in place of the shack, the finest house in the world. It had large windows and every room was filled with furniture. By spring, the mill had ground out the last thing that was needed for the house, and the poor brother cried,

"Halt, halt, little mill!"
The mill obeyed him.

Soon the poor brother had everything that he wanted. He placed the mill behind the kitchen door and sat down with his wife to eat the finest food he had ever tasted.

The following year, a rich merchant sailed from a distant land and anchored his ship in the harbor. He visited the home of the poor brother and asked about the mill, for he had heard how wonderful it was. "Will it grind salt?" the merchant asked. "Yes, indeed!" said the poor brother. "It will grind anything in the whole world except snow and meat."

"Let me borrow the mill for a short time," said the merchant. He thought it would be much easier to fill his ship with salt from the mill, than to make a long voyage across the ocean to buy salt for the people of his land. Tony agreed and the merchant went away with the mill. He did not wait to find out how to stop the grinding. When the merchant went aboard the ship, he said to the captain, "Here is a great treasure. Guard it carefully."

When they were out at sea, the merchant said, "Captain, we need not go any further upon our voyage. The mill will grind out salt enough to fill the entire ship."

So saying, he cried,

"Grind, quickly grind, little mill,

Grind SALT—with a right good will!"

And the mill ground salt, and more salt, and still more salt. When the ship was full of salt, the merchant cried, "Now you must stop, little mill." The little mill did not stop. It kept on grinding salt, and more salt, and still more salt. The captain shouted, "We shall be lost! The ship will sink!" One of the sailors called, "Ahoy, captain! Throw the mill overboard." So, heave ho! Heave ho! And overboard went the wonderful mill, down to the bottom of the deep sea. The captain and his crew sailed home with the merchant's cargo of salt. The mill kept on grinding salt at the bottom of the sea.

AND THAT IS WHY THE SEA IS SALTY.

At least, that's what some people say.

16. What did the rich brother give to the poor brother?　　　　　　　3R3J
　　A. porridge　　　　B. meat　　　　　C. gold　　　　　D. snow

17. The first paragraph says, "The wind howled outside and the snow almost cov-　3R3F
　　ered the tiny shack..." What time of year is it when the story starts??
　　A. summer　　　　　　　　　C. winter
　　B. fall　　　　　　　　　　　D. spring

18. What did the dwarfs give to the poor brother?　　　　　　　3R3J
　　A. snow　　　　　B. a mill　　　　C. some meat　　　D. plenty of salt

19. How do you think Tony feels now that he has everything he needs?　3R3B
　　A. jealous　　　B. mad　　　　C. sad　　　　D. overjoyed

20. This passage can best be described as   3R3N
    A. nonfiction
    C. poetry
    B. drama
    D. fiction

21. What is a synonym for the word *voyage*?   3R2C
    A. trip
    B. boat
    C. ocean
    D. cave

22. What happened FIRST in this story?   3R3E
    A. Tony got a new house.
    B. The dwarfs gave the mill to Tony.
    C. The mill was thrown overboard.
    D. Ted gave his poor brother meat.

23. What happened LAST in this story?   3R3E
    A. Tony got a new house.
    B. The dwarfs gave the mill to Tony.
    C. The mill was thrown overboard.
    D. Ted gave his poor brother mea.t

24. What is this story MAINLY about?   3R3G
    A. It tells people how to mill products.
    B. It informs readers about dwarfs.
    C. It explains why the sea is salty.
    D. It talks about the many uses of salt.

25. In the first paragraph, what does the word *stingy* mean?   3R2F
    A. happy
    B. selfish
    C. skinny
    D. generous

26. Who heard that the poor brother owned the mill?   3R3M
    A. a sailor
    B. a dwarf
    C. a merchant
    D. a woman

27. According to this story, why is the sea salty? 3R3L
    A. because the dwarfs put salt into the sea
    B. because the mill was thrown overboard still making salt
    C. because the poor brother wanted the sea salty
    D. because the ship sank and all its salt went into the sea

28. Where does this story MOST LIKELY take place? 3R3E, F
    A. on another planet
    B. in the mountains
    C. in a town near the sea
    D. on a tropical island

Read this passage, then answer the questions.

Homework Blues

BELLA: (picks up cell phone and dials) Hello, Fairy Godmother?

Fairy Godmother: (answers cell phone from secret pocket) Hello, dear.

BELLA: Is this my Fairy Godmother?

FAIRY GODMOTHER: Yes. What's the problem, dear?

BELLA: It's my parents. When I come home from school they want me to do my homework before I go out and play, but by the time I finish my homework it's, dinnertime, and by the time dinner's over, it's dark, and then I have to get ready for bed, and there's no time to play in the yard except on weekends. I don't think it's fair. I need your help, please.

FAIRY GODMOTHER: Well, maybe you could make a deal. Why don't you tell your parents that you promise to do your homework after dinner if you can play outside before dinner?

BELLA: Great idea, Fairy Godmother! I'll ask them tonight.

(This is the end of the first conversation.)

BELLA: (dials cell phone again) Hello, Fairy Godmother?

FAIRY GODMOTHER: Yes, dear?

BELLA: Your idea did not work.

FAIRY GODMOTHER: Whatever do you mean? I can't imagine that!

BELLA: Well, I made a deal with my parents, and they let me play outside before dinner, but when I did my homework after dinner, it took so long that I didn't get to bed on time. My parents got real grumpy. They said your idea didn't work and I'll have to go back to doing my homework as soon as I come home from school. Can you please help me?

FAIRY GODMOTHER: Yes, of course, dear. How long does it take for you to do your homework?

BELLA: About 30 minutes every night. Or sometimes maybe a whole hour because it takes so long to settle down and do it because I am feeling so mad about not being able to play outside.

FAIRY GODMOTHER: If you get to work right away, you could finish it then in 30 minutes. You'd have the rest of the time to play, and everyone would be a lot happier. Wait a minute! I've got a better idea. How long do you spend on the school bus in the afternoon?

BELLA: About twenty minutes.

FAIRY GODMOTHER: Great! Why don't you get started on your homework while you are riding the bus home?

BELLA: Well, OK. I guess I could try that idea.

(This ends the second conversation.)

BELLA: Hello, Fairy Godmother?

FAIRY GODMOTHER: Yes, dear?

BELLA: I have great news! I started working on my homework on the school bus. When I got home, it only took me ten minutes to finish it. I had the rest of the time to go outside and play. I finished right away so that I could play outside longer. I didn't realize how much time I was wasting by complaining when I could have been outside playing. Thank you so much for your help.

FAIRY GODMOTHER: Anytime, dear. That's my job. You may call anytime.

29. What was Bella's conflict in this passage?   3R3E
   A. She did not want to ride the school bus.
   B. She missed her Fairy Godmother.
   C. She wanted to play outside and she had homework.
   D. She wanted another afternoon snack.

30. What was Bella supposed to do after dinner?   3R3J
   A. play outside
   B. read books
   C. get ready for bed
   D. ride the school bus

31. What is a synonym for the word *grumpy*?   3R2C
   A. cranky   B. happy   C. sad   D. confused

Practice Test 2

Tea and Cakes for Sisters

Mrs. Hubbard and Mrs. Dowless are sisters. Mrs. Hubbard lives in a house in Atlanta and Mrs. Dowless lives in an apartment in Macon. One day Mrs. Hubbard visited her sister. When her sister answered the door, Mrs. Hubbard saw tears in her eyes. "What's the matter?" she asked. Mrs. Dowless said "I am so lonely. We never get to see each other. What can we do?"

She began to cry again. Mrs. Hubbard was very sad because she missed her sister, too. Suddenly Mrs. Hubbard said, "Why don't we make sure we see each other once a week for tea and cakes." Mrs. Dowless stopped crying, and the two sisters had tea together and a nice visit. They decided that they would see each other every Monday. They would take turns on driving to Atlanta or to Macon.

It was late in the afternoon, and Mrs. Hubbard had to go home. She put on her hat, coat, and gloves. Mrs. Dowless put her famous lemon squares into a small shopping bag for her sister to take home. Mrs. Hubbard took the shopping bag and thanked her sister. She stopped at a rest area on the way home to stretch her legs and use the restroom. She took the lemon squares with her so that they would not melt in the car. She put the bag down by the sink to wash her hands. Then, she went outside and took a short walk around the nature trail. Suddenly she remembered she left the shopping bag by the sink.

32. Where does Mrs. Hubbard live? 3R3M
    A. Macon   B. Atlanta   C. Marietta   D. Dalton

33. What does Mrs. Dowless do when Mrs. Hubbard arrives? 3R3M
    A. gives her a big hug   C. walks away
    B. cries   D. kisses her cheek

34. Why did Mrs. Hubbard stop on the way home? 3R3L
    A. to get more gas   C. to use the restroom
    B. to drop off a package   D. to take a nap

35. How did the sisters solve their problem? 3R3L
    A. They decided not see each other for awhile.
    B. They decided to see each other every week.
    C. They decided to meet downtown.
    D. They took a drive together.

36. At the end of the passage, what will MOST LIKELY happen next? 3R3B
    A. Someone will eat the lemon squares and leave a note.
    B. Mrs. Hubbard will get the lemon squares and go home.
    C. Mrs. Hubbard will drive back to her sister's house for more lemon squares.
    D. Mrs. Hubbard's car won't start.

Look at this information, and then answer the questions that follow.

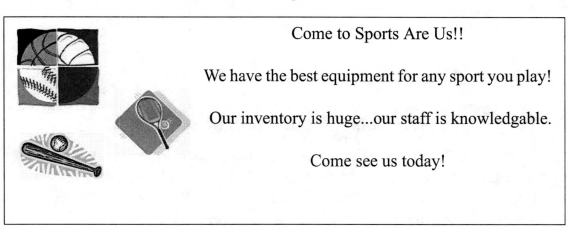

Come to Sports Are Us!!

We have the best equipment for any sport you play!

Our inventory is huge...our staff is knowledgable.

Come see us today!

37. What genre of writing is this? 3R3N
    A. poetry   B. drama   C. fiction   D. nonfiction

38. From the pictures, which equipment is something that Sports Are Us might 3R3H
    NOT have?
    A. ice skates   C. tennis rackets
    B. basketballs   D. soccer balls

39. What does this passage tell readers? 3R3G
    A. It invites readers to shop at Sports Are Us.
    B. It educates readers about various sports.
    C. It shows what equipment is needed for sports.
    D. It describes why good equipment is important to have.

40. Why did someone write this passage?   3R3P
    A. to convince people to play more sports
    B. to teach the rules of basketball and baseball
    C. to persuade people to shop at this store
    D. to tell a funny story about a tennis match

41. What word in the passage has a **suffix** that means "able to"?   3R2E
    A. equipment   C. knowledgable
    B. inventory   D. today

Read this passage. Answer the questions after it.

Welcome to the World of Spiders

Spiders belong to a special group of animals called invertebrates. An invertebrate is any animal that does not have a backbone. Animals that have a backbone are called vertebrates. Insects, sea shells, worms, and octopuses are some other animals that do not have backbones.

Spiders are a special kind of invertebrate. Spiders are not insects. People make the mistake that spiders are insects, but this is not true. They belong to a group of invertebrates called arachnids. Arachnids are soft-bodied animals that have eight legs. Insects have only six legs. Spiders are not insects because they have eight legs.

42. What does the word *invertebrate* mean?   3R2B, F
    A. any animal that is an insect
    B. a definition for a spider
    C. an animal without a backbone
    D. a shy person

43. Which word has a **prefix** that means "wrongly" or "badly"?   3R2E
    A. invertibrate   B. insect   C. arachnid   D. mistake

44. What is the author's purpose in this passage?   3R3P
    A. to educate readers about the spider group
    B. to inform readers about insects
    C. to inform readers about the many different kinds of spiders
    D. to educate readers about how to treat spider bites

45. A ladybug would be   3R3J
    A. an insect.
    B. a vertibrate.
    C. an arachnid.
    D. too small to worry about.

Read this passage. Then answer the questions that follow.

Little Black

In Kentucky, there was a stable which was the home of four horses. The four horses were named Lightning, Jack, Big Red, and Little Black. Lightning was the most popular horse to ride because he rode very fast. Jack was also fun to ride because he was very easy-going and never complained about anything. Big Red was mighty and quick, and he was always up for a run. Little Black was a small horse that had a problem. He was not picked often to ride because he was very clumsy. He was always bumping into things like trees, fences, and bales of hay on the farm.

One day, four girls came to ride the horses. They saddled up and headed out into the meadow. Little Black was so excited to be going on this special trip. The horses came across a large bale of hay. Lightning and Jack jumped over the haybale. Big Red walked around it, but Little Black rode right into it and got hay all over himself and his rider, Jessica. "Oh no," cried Jessica, "now my jeans are covered in hay."

Next, the horses came to a large mud puddle. Lightning and Jack jumped over the mud puddle. Big Red walked around the mud puddle. And what do you think happened next? Little Black did not see the mud puddle and he ran right through it. "Oh no," cried Jessica, "now my jeans are covered in mud. This horse even got mud in my hair."

Next, they came to a rocky stream that they had to cross. Lightning, Jack, and Big Red made their way across very smoothly. That did not happen to Little Black. He began to cross, and as he put his right foot out, he slipped on a mossy rock and fell into the water. "Oh no," cried Jessica, "now I am soaking wet. This horse is not a good riding horse at all!"

Jessica wanted to go back to the stable immediately. As they were riding back, she noticed that Little Black kept squinting his eyes. Jessica had just been to the eye doctor for the first time because she had been squinting her eyes. Her teacher suggested that she might have a vision problem. Sometimes, Jessica could not see all of the letters and numbers on the board. She led Little Black toward the fence and sure enough Little Black ran right into the fence. Jessica could not believe it. She felt sure that Little Black was not clumsy on purpose. She thought that Little Black was having difficulty seeing things.

When they got back to the stable, she talked to the stable owner. He was so excited when Jessica told him about her discovery. Jessica showed Little Black her new pink glasses and comforted Little Black. He was feeling blue because he made so many mistakes on the trip. Jessica promised to visit him every week. They became good friends.

46. Who is the main character in this story? 3R3E, F
    A. Lightning   B. Jack   C. Little Black   D. Big Red

47. Where does this story MOSTLY take place? 3R3E
    A. near a stream
    B. in the stable
    C. in the meadow
    D. near a lake

48. What happened FIRST on the ride? 3R3F
    A. Little Black tripped over a bale of hay.
    B. Little Black fell down.
    C. Little Black ran through a mud puddle.
    D. Little Black ran into a fence.

49. Which of these is an opinion?   3R3D
    A. Little Black ran through a mud puddle.
    B. Little Black should not be taking riders.
    C. Little Black kept squinting his eyes.
    D. Little Black ran into a fence.

50. What can you conclude about Little Black?   3R3L
    A. He does not like taking people on rides.
    B. He will never be used for riding again.
    C. He needs to get special glasses for horses.
    D. He is clumsy, and it has nothing to do with his eyesight.

Practice Test 2